BURGERS

Table of Contents

Great Grilled Burgers with Spinach Pesto

Spinach Pesto (recipe follows)
1½ pounds ground beef
¼ teaspoon salt
¼ teaspoon black pepper
4 to 8 slices provolone cheese
4 crusty Italian rolls, split and toasted
Red leaf lettuce
Tomato slices

1. Prepare grill for direct cooking. Prepare Spinach Pesto.

2. Combine beef, ¼ cup pesto, salt and pepper in large bowl; mix lightly. Shape into 4 patties about ¾ inch thick.

3. Grill patties, covered, over medium heat 8 to 10 minutes or until cooked through (160°F), turning once. Top with cheese during last 2 minutes of grilling.

4. Spread remaining pesto on cut sides of rolls. Serve burgers on rolls with lettuce and tomato. *Makes 4 servings*

Spinach Pesto: Combine 2 cups spinach leaves, 3 tablespoons grated Romano cheese, 3 tablespoons olive oil, 1 tablespoon dried basil, 1 tablespoon lemon juice and 3 cloves garlic in food processor or blender; process until smooth. Makes about ½ cup.

Classic California Burgers

 2 tablespoons *French's*® Honey Dijon Mustard
 2 tablespoons mayonnaise
 2 tablespoons sour cream
 1 pound ground beef
 2 tablespoons *French's*® Worcestershire Sauce
 1⅓ cups *French's*® Cheddar or Original French Fried Onions, divided
 ½ teaspoon garlic salt
 ¼ teaspoon ground black pepper
 4 hamburger rolls, split and toasted
 ½ small avocado, sliced
 ½ cup sprouts

1. Combine mustard, mayonnaise and sour cream; set aside.

2. Combine beef, Worcestershire, *⅔ cup* French Fried Onions and seasonings. Form into 4 patties. Grill over high heat until juices run clear (160°F internal temperature).

3. Place burgers on rolls. Top each with mustard sauce, avocado slices, sprouts and remaining onions, dividing evenly. Cover with top halves of rolls. *Makes 4 servings*

BBQ Cheese Burgers: Top each burger with 1 slice American cheese, 1 tablespoon barbecue sauce and 2 tablespoons French Fried Onions.

Pizza Burgers: Top each burger with pizza sauce, mozzarella cheese and French Fried Onions.

Prep Time: 10 minutes | Cook Time: 10 minutes

Mouthwatering Beef

Classic California Burger

Bacon and Blue Cheese Stuffed Burgers

4 slices applewood-smoked bacon or regular bacon
1 small red onion, finely chopped
2 tablespoons crumbled blue cheese
1 tablespoon butter, softened
1½ pounds ground beef
   Salt and black pepper
4 onion or plain hamburger rolls
   Lettuce leaves

1. Cook bacon in large skillet over medium-high heat until chewy. Transfer to paper towels. Chop bacon into small pieces. Add onion to same skillet; cook until tender. Cool slightly.

2. Combine bacon, onion, blue cheese and butter in small bowl; mix well. Prepare grill for direct cooking.

3. Divide ground beef into 8 thin patties about 4 inches wide; season with salt and pepper. Place 2 tablespoons bacon mixture in center of one patty; cover with second patty. Pinch edges together to seal. Repeat with remaining patties and cheese mixture.

4. Grill patties, covered, over medium heat 8 to 10 minutes or until cooked through (160°F), turning once. Transfer burgers to platter; let stand 2 minutes before serving. Serve burgers on rolls with lettuce.

Makes 4 servings

> **TIP:** If you want juicy, flavorful burgers, do not flatten patties while grilling. Pressing down on the patties with a spatula not only squeezes out tasty juices, but in this recipe it might also cause the stuffing to pop out.

Bacon and Blue Cheese Stuffed Burger

Parmesan Honey Lager Burgers

1½ **pounds ground beef**
¾ **cup honey lager, divided**
⅓ **cup grated Parmesan cheese**
1 **tablespoon Worcestershire sauce**
¼ **teaspoon black pepper**
3 **tablespoons mayonnaise**
3 **tablespoons ketchup**
½ **teaspoon yellow mustard**
4 **hamburger buns**
8 **tomato slices**
8 **red onion slices**

1. Prepare grill for direct cooking.

2. Combine beef, ¼ cup lager, Parmesan cheese, Worcestershire sauce and pepper in large bowl; mix lightly. Shape into 4 patties.

3. Combine mayonnaise, ketchup, 1 tablespoon lager and mustard in small bowl; mix well.

4. Grill patties over medium-high heat 3 minutes; turn and brush with some of remaining lager. Grill 3 minutes; turn and brush with lager. Repeat grilling and brushing until cooked through (160°F).

5. Spread mayonnaise mixture on cut sides of buns. Serve burgers on buns with tomatoes and onions.   *Makes 4 servings*

Parmesan Honey Lager Burger

Western Barbecue Burgers with Beer Barbecue Sauce

1½ pounds ground beef
1 cup smokehouse-style barbecue sauce
¼ cup brown ale
½ teaspoon salt
¼ teaspoon black pepper
1 red onion, cut into ½-inch-thick slices
4 hamburger buns
8 thick slices bacon, cooked until crisp
Lettuce leaves
Tomato slices

1. Prepare grill for direct cooking. Shape beef into 4 patties about ¾ inch thick. Cover and refrigerate.

2. Combine barbecue sauce, ale, salt and pepper in small saucepan. Bring to a boil; boil 1 minute. Remove from heat.

3. Grill onion over medium-high heat 4 minutes or until softened and slightly charred, turning occasionally. Grill patties, covered, over medium heat 8 to 10 minutes or until cooked through (160°F), turning once.

4. Serve burgers on buns with onion, bacon, barbecue sauce mixture, lettuce and tomato.   *Makes 4 servings*

Western Barbecue Burger with Beer Barbecue Sauce

Audacious Two-Cheese Burgers

1½ pounds ground beef
⅓ cup chopped fresh Italian parsley
1 tablespoon Dijon mustard
1 tablespoon Worcestershire sauce
¾ teaspoon black pepper, divided
½ teaspoon dried thyme
½ thinly sliced English cucumber
3 slices red onion, separated into rings
4 radishes, thinly sliced
1 tablespoon olive oil
1 teaspoon red wine vinegar
¼ teaspoon salt
4 slices Cheddar cheese
4 slices Gouda cheese
4 whole wheat rolls, split and toasted
Lettuce leaves

1. Prepare grill for direct cooking. Combine beef, parsley, mustard, Worcestershire sauce, ½ teaspoon pepper and thyme in large bowl; mix lightly. Shape into 4 patties about ¾ inch thick. Cover and refrigerate.

2. Combine cucumber, onion, radishes, oil, vinegar, salt and remaining ¼ teaspoon pepper in small bowl; mix well.

3. Grill patties, covered, over medium heat 8 to 10 minutes or until cooked through (160°F), turning once. Top burgers with Cheddar cheese during last 2 minutes of grilling.

4. Layer Gouda cheese, cucumber mixture, lettuce and burgers on rolls.

Makes 4 servings

Audacious Two-Cheese Burger

Gourmet Burgers with Pancetta and Gorgonzola

1½ **pounds ground beef**
2 **ounces (about ½ cup) Gorgonzola or blue cheese crumbles**
2 **tablespoons mayonnaise**
1 **red bell pepper, quartered**
4 **thick slices red onion**
   Salt and black pepper
4 **egg or brioche rolls, split and toasted**
   Red leaf lettuce
4 **to 8 slices pancetta or bacon, cooked until crisp**

1. Prepare grill for direct cooking. Shape beef into 4 patties about ¾ inch thick. Cover and refrigerate. Combine cheese and mayonnaise in small bowl; refrigerate until ready to serve.

2. Grill bell pepper and onion, covered, over medium-high heat 8 to 10 minutes or until browned, turning once. (Use grill basket, if desired.) Transfer to plate; keep warm.

3. Grill patties, covered, over medium heat 8 to 10 minutes or until cooked through (160°F), turning once. Season with salt and black pepper.

4. Spread cheese mixture on cut sides of rolls. Serve burgers on rolls with pancetta, onion and bell pepper.   *Makes 4 servings*

Zesty Chipotle Cheddar Burgers

2 pounds lean ground beef
2 cups medium salsa, divided
1 cup green onions, chopped and divided
1 cup tortilla chips, finely crushed and divided
1 tablespoon garlic salt
1 tablespoon chili powder
8 hamburger buns, split
8 slices SARGENTO® Deli Style Sliced Chipotle Cheddar Cheese

1. Combine ground beef, 1 cup salsa, ½ cup green onions, ½ cup tortilla chips, garlic salt and chili powder in large bowl. Shape beef mixture into 8 patties, 4 inches in diameter and ½ inch thick. Preheat grill or broiler.

2. Grill patties 5 minutes each side or until no longer pink in center (see Tip). Grill or lightly toast hamburger buns. Top patties with 1 slice cheese before removing from grill or broiler; let melt.

3. Place patties on buns. Top with remaining salsa, tortilla chips and green onions. *Makes 8 burgers*

Cook Time: 10 minutes

> ▌ **TIP:** For food safety, use a food thermometer to assure the internal temperature of the burgers is at least 160°F (the temperature of medium-done meat).

Deluxe Bacon & Gouda Burgers

1½ pounds ground beef
⅓ cup mayonnaise
1 teaspoon minced garlic
¼ teaspoon Dijon mustard
4 thick red onion slices
    Salt and pepper
4 to 8 slices Gouda cheese
4 onion rolls, split and toasted
    Bibb lettuce leaves
    Tomato slices
4 to 8 slices bacon, cooked until crisp

1. Prepare grill for direct cooking. Shape beef into 4 patties about ¾ inch thick. Cover and refrigerate.

2. Combine mayonnaise, garlic and mustard in small bowl; mix well.

3. Grill patties, covered, over medium heat 8 to 10 minutes or until cooked through (160°F), turning once. Remove onion when slightly browned. Season burgers with salt and pepper. Top burgers with cheese during last 2 minutes of grilling.

4. Spread mayonnaise mixture on cut sides of rolls. Serve burgers on rolls with tomato, onion and bacon.   *Makes 4 servings*

Substitution: To save time, substitute a prepared mayonnaise spread for the garlic mayonnaise.

Deluxe Bacon & Gouda Burger

Ranchero Onion Burgers

  1 pound ground beef
½ cup salsa
½ cup (2 ounces) shredded Monterey Jack cheese
1⅓ cups *French's*® Cheddar or Original French Fried Onions, divided
½ teaspoon garlic powder
¼ teaspoon ground black pepper
  4 hamburger rolls

1. Combine beef, salsa, cheese, ⅔ *cup* French Fried Onions, garlic powder and pepper in large bowl. Shape into 4 patties.

2. Place patties on oiled grid. Grill* over medium coals 10 minutes or until no longer pink in center, turning once. Serve on rolls. Garnish with Salsa Olé, if desired. Top with remaining ⅔ *cup* onions.

Makes 4 servings

*Or broil 6 inches from heat.

Tip: For extra-crispy warm onion flavor, heat French Fried Onions in the microwave for 1 minute. Or place in a foil pan and heat on the grill 2 minutes.

Salsa Olé: Combine 1½ cups prepared salsa with ¼ cup *Frank's® Redhot®* Hot Sauce.

Prep Time: 10 minutes | Cook Time: 10 minutes

Mouthwatering Beef

Ranchero Onion Burger

Brie Burgers with Sun-Dried Tomato and Artichoke Spread

1½ pounds ground beef
½ cup sun-dried tomatoes packed in oil, drained and chopped
¼ cup chopped shallots
1 tablespoon plus 1 teaspoon minced garlic, divided
1 teaspoon black pepper, divided
½ teaspoon salt, divided
1 cup canned quartered artichokes, drained and chopped
2 tablespoons mayonnaise
¼ pound Brie, sliced
2 tablespoons butter, softened
4 egg or Kaiser rolls, split
Arugula or lettuce leaves
Heirloom tomato slices

1. Prepare grill for direct cooking.

2. Combine beef, half of sun-dried tomatoes, shallots, 1 tablespoon garlic, ½ teaspoon pepper and ¼ teaspoon salt in large bowl; mix lightly. Shape into 4 patties about ¾ inch thick. Cover and refrigerate.

3. Combine remaining half of sun-dried tomatoes, artichokes, mayonnaise, remaining 1 teaspoon garlic, ½ teaspoon pepper and ¼ teaspoon salt in small bowl; mix well.

4. Grill patties, covered, over medium heat 8 to 10 minutes or until cooked through (160°F), turning once. Top burgers with cheese during last 2 minutes of grilling.

5. Spread butter on cut sides of rolls. Grill rolls until lightly browned. Spread artichoke mixture on bottom halves of rolls. Serve burgers on rolls with arugula and tomato. *Makes 4 servings*

Brie Burger with Sun-Dried Tomato and Artichoke Spread

The All-American Burger

    Burger Spread (recipe follows)
1½ pounds ground beef
  2 tablespoons chopped fresh Italian parsley
  2 teaspoons onion powder
  2 teaspoons Worcestershire sauce
  1 teaspoon garlic powder
  1 teaspoon salt
  1 teaspoon black pepper
  4 hamburger buns, split
    Lettuce leaves

1. Prepare grill for direct cooking. Prepare Burger Spread.

2. Combine beef, parsley, onion powder, Worcestershire sauce, garlic powder, salt and pepper in medium bowl; mix lightly. Shape into 4 patties about ¾ inch thick.

3. Grill patties, covered, over medium heat 8 to 10 minutes or until cooked through (160°F), turning once.

4. Serve burgers on buns with lettuce and Burger Spread.

Makes 4 servings

Burger Spread

½ cup ketchup
¼ cup mustard
2 tablespoons chopped onion
1 tablespoon relish or chopped pickles
1 tablespoon chopped fresh Italian parsley

Combine ketchup, mustard, onion, relish and parsley in small bowl; mix well.

Makes 1 cup

The All-American Burger

Southwest Pesto Burgers

½ cup fresh cilantro, stemmed
1½ teaspoons chopped jalapeño pepper*
1 clove garlic
¾ teaspoon salt, divided
¼ cup vegetable oil
2 tablespoons mayonnaise
1¼ pounds ground beef
4 slices pepper jack cheese
4 Kaiser rolls
1 ripe avocado, sliced
Salsa

Jalapeño peppers can sting and irritate the skin, so wear rubber gloves when handling peppers and do not touch your eyes.

1. Combine cilantro, jalapeño, garlic and ¼ teaspoon salt in food processor; process until garlic is minced. Slowly add oil with motor running; process until thick paste forms.

2. Prepare grill for direct cooking. Combine mayonnaise and 1 tablespoon pesto in small bowl; mix well.

3. Combine beef, remaining ¼ cup pesto and ½ teaspoon salt in large bowl; mix lightly. Shape into 4 patties.

4. Grill patties, covered, over medium heat 8 to 10 minutes or until cooked through (160°F), turning once. Top burgers with cheese during last 2 minutes of grilling.

5. Spread mayonnaise mixture on cut sides of rolls. Serve burgers on rolls with avocado and salsa.   *Makes 4 servings*

Southwest Pesto Burger

Beef and Mushroom Burger

1½ pounds extra-lean ground beef
1 small onion, minced
3 tablespoons fresh parsley
¼ cup light mayonnaise
1 tablespoon MRS. DASH® Tomato Basil Garlic Seasoning Blend
1 tablespoon Dijon mustard
6 portobello mushrooms
4 tablespoons MRS. DASH® Steak Grilling Blend™, divided
6 hamburger buns, split

1. Mix ground beef, onion and parsley in a bowl. Shape into 6 burgers.

2. Mix mayonnaise, MRS. DASH® Tomato Basil Garlic and mustard in a small bowl and set aside. Preheat grill to medium.

3. Remove stems from mushrooms and brush with water. Sprinkle with 1 tablespoon MRS. DASH® Steak Grilling Blend™. Place remaining MRS. DASH® Steak Grilling Blend™ on a plate and pat burgers into it on both sides.

4. Grill burgers and mushrooms, turning once, until mushrooms are browned and tender and the burgers reach 160°F.

5. Grill buns until toasted. Place each burger on a bun and top with a mushroom and reserved sauce.   *Makes 6 servings*

Prep Time: 10 minutes | Cook Time: 15 to 16 minutes

Caesar Salad Beef Burgers on Garlic Crostini

1½ pounds ground beef
3 cloves garlic, minced
1 teaspoon salt
½ teaspoon pepper
4 Romaine lettuce leaves
¼ cup freshly shaved or grated Parmesan cheese

GARLIC CROSTINI

8 slices sourdough bread (about 4×3×½ inch)
Extra-virgin olive oil
2 large cloves garlic, cut lengthwise into quarters

1. Combine ground beef, minced garlic, 1 teaspoon salt and ½ teaspoon pepper in large bowl, mixing lightly but thoroughly. Lightly shape into four ¾-inch-thick patties, shaping to fit the bread slices.

2. Place patties on grid over medium, ash-covered coals. Grill, uncovered, 13 to 15 minutes (over medium heat on preheated gas grill, covered, 13 to 14 minutes) until instant-read thermometer inserted horizontally into center registers 160°F, turning occasionally. Season with salt and pepper, as desired.

3. Meanwhile, brush both sides of bread slices lightly with oil. Place bread around outer edge of grid. Grill a few minutes until lightly toasted, turning once. Remove bread slices from grid; rub both sides of each slice with a garlic quarter.

4. Place one lettuce leaf on four of the bread slices; top each with a burger. Sprinkle evenly with cheese; cover with remaining bread slices. Cut burgers in half; arrange on lettuce-lined platter, if desired.

Makes 4 servings

Tip: Use a vegetable peeler to quickly shave Parmesan cheese.

Prep and Cook Time: **30 minutes**

Favorite recipe courtesy of *The Beef Checkoff*

Backyard Barbecue Burgers

1½ pounds ground beef
⅓ cup barbecue sauce, divided
1 onion, cut into thick slices
1 to 2 tomatoes, cut into slices
1 to 2 tablespoons olive oil
4 kaiser rolls, split and toasted
Green lettuce leaves

1. Prepare grill for direct cooking.

2. Combine ground beef and 2 tablespoons barbecue sauce in large bowl. Shape into 4 patties about 1 inch thick.

3. Grill patties, covered, over medium heat 8 to 10 minutes or until cooked through (160°F), turning once. Brush both sides with remaining barbecue sauce during last 5 minutes of grilling.

4. Meanwhile, brush onion and tomato with oil. Grill onion 10 minutes or until tender and charred. Grill tomato 2 to 3 minutes.

5. Serve burgers on rolls with tomato, onion and lettuce.

Makes 4 servings

Backyard Barbecue Burger

Grilled Reuben Burger

    1 envelope LIPTON® RECIPE SECRETS® Onion Soup Mix*
    ½ cup water
  1½ pounds ground beef
    ½ cup shredded Swiss cheese (about 2 ounces)
    1 tablespoon crisp-cooked crumbled bacon or bacon bits
    ½ teaspoon caraway seeds (optional)

Also terrific with LIPTON® RECIPE SECRETS® Onion Mushroom Soup Mix.

1. In large bowl, combine all ingredients; shape into 6 patties.

2. Grill or broil until done. Top, if desired, with heated sauerkraut and additional bacon.   *Makes 6 servings*

Welsh Rarebit Pub Style Burgers

  1½ pounds ground beef
    1 can CAMPBELL'S® Cheddar Cheese Soup
    ¼ cup water
    1 tablespoon Worcestershire sauce
    1 teaspoon prepared mustard
    6 English muffins, split and toasted

1. Shape beef into 6 patties, ½ inch thick.

2. Cook patties in a skillet until browned. Pour off fat.

3. Add soup, water, Worcestershire and mustard. Heat to a boil. Cover and cook over low heat 5 minutes or until done.

4. Serve on muffins with sauce.   *Makes 6 servings*

Prep and Cook Time: 20 minutes

Grilled Reuben Burger

Beyond Beef

Chutney Turkey Burgers

1 pound ground turkey
½ cup prepared chutney, divided
½ teaspoon salt
½ teaspoon black pepper
⅛ teaspoon hot pepper sauce
½ cup nonfat plain yogurt
1 teaspoon curry powder
4 hamburger buns, split

1. Preheat grill for direct cooking.

2. In medium bowl, combine turkey, ¼ cup chutney, salt, black pepper and hot pepper sauce. Shape turkey mixture into 4 burgers approximately 3½ inches in diameter. Grill turkey burgers 5 to 6 minutes per side or until 165°F is reached on meat thermometer and turkey is no longer pink in center.

3. In small bowl, combine yogurt, curry powder and remaining ¼ cup chutney.

4. To serve, place burgers on bottom halves of buns; spoon yogurt mixture over burgers and cover with top halves of buns.

Makes 4 servings

Favorite recipe from *National Turkey Federation*

Chicken Burgers with White Cheddar

1¼ pounds ground chicken
1 cup plain dry bread crumbs
½ cup diced red bell pepper
½ cup ground walnuts
¼ cup sliced green onions
¼ cup light beer
2 tablespoons chopped fresh Italian parsley
2 tablespoons lemon juice
2 cloves garlic, minced
¾ teaspoon salt
⅛ teaspoon black pepper
Nonstick cooking spray
4 slices white Cheddar cheese
4 whole wheat buns
Dijon mustard
Lettuce leaves

1. Combine chicken, bread crumbs, bell pepper, walnuts, green onions, beer, parsley, lemon juice, garlic, salt and black pepper in large bowl; mix lightly. Shape into 4 patties.

2. Spray large skillet with cooking spray; heat over medium-high heat. Cook patties 12 to 14 minutes or until cooked through (165°F), turning once. Top burgers with cheese. Cover skillet; cook 1 minute or just until cheese melts.

3. Serve burgers on buns with mustard and lettuce. *Makes 4 servings*

Chicken Burger with White Cheddar

Deluxe Mediterranean Lamb Burgers

1½ pounds ground lamb
  1 tablespoon minced garlic
  2 teaspoons Greek seasoning
  1 teaspoon paprika
  ½ teaspoon salt, divided
  ½ teaspoon black pepper
  4 thin red onion slices, separated into rings
  1 tablespoon olive oil
  1 teaspoon chopped fresh mint or Italian parsley
  1 teaspoon red wine vinegar
    Spinach leaves
  4 whole grain rolls, split and toasted
  4 to 8 tomato slices
  1 package (4 ounces) feta cheese crumbles

1. Prepare grill for direct cooking.

2. Combine lamb, garlic, seasoning, paprika, ¼ teaspoon salt and pepper in large bowl; mix lightly. Shape into 4 patties about ¾ inch thick. Cover and refrigerate.

3. Combine onion, oil, mint, vinegar and remaining ¼ teaspoon salt in small bowl; toss to coat.

4. Grill patties, covered, over medium heat 8 to 10 minutes or until cooked through (160°F), turning once.

5. Serve burgers on rolls with spinach, tomato, onion mixture and feta cheese. *Makes 4 servings*

Deluxe Mediterranean Lamb Burger

Barbecued Turkey Burgers

    1 package JENNIE-O TURKEY STORE® Ground Turkey
    ¼ cup prepared barbecue sauce
    2 tablespoons dry bread crumbs
    4 whole grain sandwich buns

CLASSIC COLESLAW
    2 cups thinly shredded cabbage
    ¼ cup *each* shredded carrot and thinly sliced red onion
    3 tablespoons reduced-calorie mayonnaise
    2 teaspoons *each* lime juice and granulated sugar

In medium bowl, combine turkey, barbecue sauce and bread crumbs; mix lightly. Shape into 4 patties (½ inch thick). Grill over hot coals, 4 inches from heat, until meat springs back when touched and burgers are no longer pink in center, about 4 minutes per side. Serve burgers topped with Classic Coleslaw in buns.   *Makes 4 servings*

Classic Coleslaw: In large bowl, combine cabbage, carrot, onion, mayonnaise, lime juice and sugar. Mix well. Makes about 2½ cups.

Barbecued Turkey Burgers

Chicken Fajita Burgers

1 pound ground chicken
1 slice whole wheat bread, processed into crumbs
¼ cup chopped onion
2 tablespoons *each* chopped red and green bell pepper
2 tablespoons bottled medium-hot salsa
1 egg white, lightly beaten
1 tablespoon fajita seasoning
4 whole wheat hamburger buns, split, toasted
    Mexicali Mayonnaise (recipe follows)
4 lettuce leaves
4 tomato slices
8 avocado slices (thin vertical slices)

In a large bowl, mix together ground chicken, bread crumbs, onion, peppers, salsa, egg white and fajita seasoning. Form mixture into 4 patties. Place patties on rack of broiler pan. Position pan about 6 inches from heat and broil, turning once, 10 minutes or until burgers reach an internal temperature of 170°F. Spread cut side of bottom half of each toasted bun with 1 teaspoon Mexicali Mayonnaise. Top with lettuce, burger, tomato slice, 2 avocado slices, additional mayonnaise mixture, if desired, and top half of bun. ➳ *Makes 4 servings*

Mexicali Mayonnaise: In a small bowl, mix 2 tablespoons light mayonnaise with 2 teaspoons bottled medium-hot salsa.

Favorite recipe from *Delmarva Poultry Industry, Inc.*

Bistro Burgers with Blue Cheese

    1 pound ground turkey or beef
    ¼ cup chopped fresh parsley
    2 tablespoons minced chives
    ¼ teaspoon dried thyme leaves
    2 tablespoons *French's*® Honey Dijon Mustard
       Lettuce and tomato slices
    4 crusty rolls, split in half
    2 ounces blue cheese, crumbled
 1⅓ cups *French's*® French Fried Onions

1. In large bowl, gently mix meat, herbs and mustard. Shape into 4 patties.

2. Grill or broil patties 10 minutes or until no longer pink in center. Arrange lettuce and tomatoes on bottom halves of rolls. Place burgers on top. Sprinkle with blue cheese and French Fried Onions. Cover with top halves of rolls. Serve with additional mustard.   *Makes 4 servings*

Tip: Toast onions in microwave 1 minute for extra crispness.

Prep Time: **10 minutes** | Cook Time: **10 minutes**

Savory Salmon Burgers

1 can (about 14 ounces) red salmon, drained
1 egg white
2 tablespoons toasted wheat germ
1 tablespoon dried onion flakes
1 tablespoon capers, drained
½ teaspoon dried thyme
¼ teaspoon black pepper
   Nonstick cooking spray
4 whole wheat buns, split and toasted
2 tablespoons Dijon mustard
4 tomato slices
4 thin red onion slices or dill pickle slices
   Lettuce leaves

1. Place salmon in medium bowl; mash lightly with fork. Add egg white, wheat germ, onion flakes, capers, thyme and pepper; mix well.

2. Shape mixture into 4 patties. Cover and refrigerate 1 hour or until firm.

3. Spray large skillet with cooking spray; heat over medium heat. Cook patties 10 minutes or until cooked through, turning once.

4. Spread cut sides of buns with mustard. Serve burgers on buns with tomato, onion and lettuce.   *Makes 4 servings*

> ▌ **TIP:** Red salmon is more expensive than pink salmon. It has a higher fat content, a firmer texture and is a deep red color.

Savory Salmon Burger

Grilled Salsa Turkey Burgers

½ **pound ground turkey**
2 **tablespoons salsa**
2 **tablespoons crushed tortilla chips**
2 **slices Monterey Jack cheese**
2 **whole wheat hamburger buns, split and toasted**
   Green leaf lettuce
   Additional salsa

1. Lightly spray grid with nonstick cooking spray. Prepare grill for direct cooking.

2. Combine turkey, 2 tablespoons salsa and chips in small bowl; mix lightly. Shape into 2 patties.

3. Grill patties over medium-high heat 12 minutes or until cooked through (165°F), turning once. Top burgers with cheese during last 2 minutes of grilling.

4. Serve burgers on buns with lettuce and additional salsa.

Makes 2 servings

Tip: To broil, preheat broiler. Broil patties 4 to 6 inches from heat 6 minutes per side or until cooked through (165°F).

Grilled Salsa Turkey Burger

Cubano Burgers

1½ pounds ground pork
¼ cup minced green onions
3 tablespoons yellow mustard, divided
1 tablespoon minced garlic
2 teaspoons paprika
½ teaspoon black pepper
¼ teaspoon salt
8 slices Swiss cheese
4 bolillos, split and toasted
8 slices sandwich-style dill pickles
¼ pound thinly sliced ham

1. Prepare grill for direct cooking.

2. Combine pork, green onions, 1 tablespoon mustard, garlic, paprika, pepper and salt in large bowl; mix lightly. Shape into 4 patties about ¾ inch thick.

3. Grill patties, covered, over medium heat 8 to 10 minutes or until cooked through (160°F), turning once. Top burgers with cheese during last 2 minutes of grilling.

4. Spread remaining 2 tablespoons mustard on cut sides of rolls. Layer with pickles, burgers and ham. Press down firmly.   *Makes 4 servings*

Note: Traditional Cuban sandwiches are made with sliced roast pork and do not include mayonnaise, tomatoes, onions, bell peppers or lettuce. Thinly sliced plantain chips usually accompany the sandwiches.

Substitution: A bolillo is an oval shaped roll about six inches long with a crunchy crust and a soft inside. If you can't find bolillos, use a loaf of French bread cut into individual-sized portions.

Cubano Burger

Turkey Burgers with Pesto-Red Pepper Mayonnaise

¼ cup HELLMANN'S® or BEST FOODS® Light Mayonnaise*
1 tablespoon prepared pesto
1 tablespoon finely chopped roasted red pepper
4 turkey burgers
4 Kaiser or whole grain rolls
   Tomato slices
   Lettuce leaves
   Onion slices (optional)

Also terrific with HELLMANN'S® or BEST FOODS® Low Fat Mayonnaise Dressing or Canola Cholesterol Free Mayonnaise.

Combine HELLMANN'S® or BEST FOODS® Light Mayonnaise, pesto and roasted pepper in small bowl; set aside.

Grill or broil turkey burgers 8 minutes or until thoroughly cooked, turning once. To serve, evenly spread mayonnaise mixture on rolls, then top with burgers, tomato, lettuce, onion and dollop of mayonnaise mixture.   *Makes 4 servings*

Prep Time: 10 minutes | Cook Time: 8 minutes

> ▌ **TIP:** To perk up the flavor of your burgers, mix WISH-BONE® Italian Dressing into the ground beef or ground turkey.

Turkey Burger with Pesto-Red Pepper Mayonnaise

Mediterranean Australian Lamb Burger with Goat Cheese and Tomato Relish

BURGER

1¾ pounds Australian Lamb
1 shallot, peeled and chopped
1 tablespoon capers, chopped
6 to 8 large basil leaves, sliced
   Freshly ground pepper, to taste
½ cup cornmeal (or flour), for coating
   Olive oil, for cooking

TOMATO RELISH

3 vine-ripened tomatoes, halved crosswise
1 red onion, thickly sliced
1 teaspoon sugar
1 teaspoon balsamic vinegar
   Salt and freshly ground pepper, to taste

PRESENTATION

4 Kaiser rolls or hamburger buns, split
4 tablespoons soft goat cheese (or chevre)

1. For burgers, combine ground lamb, shallot, capers, basil and pepper in a large bowl and mix well. Shape mixture into 4 burgers. Spread cornmeal over a plate and press burgers into cornmeal to coat.

2. Preheat barbecue grill or grill pan and brush with oil. Cook burgers over medium to high heat for 6 to 7 minutes or until internal temperature reaches 160°F.

3. For relish, place tomatoes flesh-side down on the grill and flip after 20 seconds, cooking until skin starts to char. Grill onions until soft; dice finely. Place in a bowl, add sugar and vinegar, season to taste with salt and pepper; mix well. Serve warm or cold.

4. Grill buns, cut side down, until lightly toasted. Spread with goat cheese and top with burgers. Serve with relish.   *Makes 4 burgers*

Favorite recipe from *Meat and Livestock Australia*

Mediterranean Australian Lamb Burger with Goat Cheese and Tomato Relish

Easy Salmon Burgers with Honey Barbecue Sauce

⅓ cup honey
⅓ cup ketchup
1½ teaspoons cider vinegar
1 teaspoon prepared horseradish
¼ teaspoon minced garlic
⅛ teaspoon red pepper flakes (optional)
1 can (7½ ounces) salmon, drained
½ cup dry bread crumbs
¼ cup chopped onion
3 tablespoons chopped green bell pepper
1 egg white
2 hamburger buns, toasted

In small bowl, combine honey, ketchup, vinegar, horseradish, garlic and red pepper flakes, if desired, until well blended. Set aside half of sauce. In separate bowl, mix together salmon, bread crumbs, onion, green pepper and egg white. Blend in 2 tablespoons remaining sauce. Divide salmon mixture into 2 patties, ½ to ¾ inch thick. Place patties on well-oiled grill, 4 to 6 inches from hot coals. Grill, turning 2 to 3 times and basting with remaining sauce, until burgers are browned and cooked through. (Or place patties on lightly greased baking sheet. Broil 4 to 6 inches from heat source, turning 2 to 3 times and basting with remaining sauce, until cooked through.) Place on hamburger buns and serve with reserved sauce. *Makes 2 servings*

Favorite recipe from *National Honey Board*

Easy Salmon Burger with Honey Barbecue Sauce

BBQ Turkey Minis

½ cup panko bread crumbs
½ cup barbecue sauce, divided
1 egg, beaten
1 pound ground turkey
1 package (12 ounces) Hawaiian bread rolls, split horizontally
Lettuce leaves
Tomato slices
3 slices American cheese, quartered

1. Lightly spray grid with nonstick cooking spray. Prepare grill for direct cooking.

2. Combine bread crumbs, ¼ cup barbecue sauce and egg in medium bowl; mix well. Add turkey; mix just until combined. Shape mixture by ¼ cupfuls into 12 patties about ½ inch thick.

3. Grill patties, covered, over medium heat 8 to 10 minutes or until cooked through (160°F), turning once. Brush with remaining ¼ cup barbecue sauce during last minute of grilling.

4. Serve burgers on rolls with tomato and cheese.

Makes 12 mini burgers

> ▌ **TIP:** The centers of turkey burgers should reach 160°F before being removed from the grill; the internal temperature will continue to rise to 165°F upon standing.

Fired-Up Buffalo Burgers

1½ pounds ground turkey
¼ cup chopped green onions
1 teaspoon paprika
1 teaspoon salt
¼ teaspoon black pepper
½ cup hot pepper sauce
⅓ cup melted butter
4 sesame seed buns, split and toasted
1 cup shredded romaine lettuce
4 to 8 tomato slices (optional)
¾ cup blue cheese dressing
¼ cup crumbled blue cheese
    Celery sticks (optional)

1. Prepare grill for direct cooking.

2. Combine turkey, green onions, paprika, salt and black pepper in large bowl; mix lightly. Shape into 4 patties about ¾ inch thick. Cover and refrigerate.

3. Combine hot pepper sauce and butter in small bowl; reserve ¼ cup mixture for dipping sauce.

4. Grill patties, covered, over medium heat 8 to 10 minutes or until cooked through (160°F), turning once. Brush patties with hot sauce mixture during last 4 minutes of grilling, turning and brushing to coat both sides.

5. Serve burgers on buns with lettuce, tomato, if desired, dressing and blue cheese. Serve with celery sticks, if desired.   *Makes 4 servings*

Lentil Burgers

1 can (about 14 ounces) vegetable broth
1 cup dried lentils, sorted and rinsed
1 carrot, grated
¼ cup coarsely chopped mushrooms
1 egg
¼ cup plain dry bread crumbs
3 tablespoons finely chopped onion
2 to 4 cloves garlic, minced
1 teaspoon dried thyme
   Nonstick cooking spray
¼ cup chopped seeded cucumber
¼ cup plain yogurt
½ teaspoon dried mint
¼ teaspoon dried dill weed
¼ teaspoon black pepper
⅛ teaspoon salt
   Dash hot pepper sauce (optional)
4 rolls
   Lettuce leaves

1. Bring broth to a boil in medium saucepan over high heat. Stir in lentils; reduce heat to low. Simmer, covered, 30 minutes or until lentils are tender and liquid is absorbed. Cool to room temperature.

2. Place lentils, carrot and mushrooms in food processor or blender; process until finely chopped but not smooth. (Some whole lentils should still be visible.) Stir in egg, bread crumbs, onion, garlic and thyme. Cover and refrigerate 2 to 3 hours.

3. Shape lentil mixture into 4 patties about ½ inch thick. Spray large skillet with nonstick cooking spray; heat over medium heat. Cook patties over medium-low heat 10 minutes or until browned on both sides, turning once.

4. Meanwhile, combine cucumber, yogurt, mint, dill weed, black pepper, salt and hot pepper sauce, if desired, in small bowl. Serve burgers on rolls with lettuce and yogurt mixture.   *Makes 4 servings*

Roasted Pepper Mushroom Burgers

3 teaspoons olive oil, divided
¾ cup thinly sliced shallots
¼ cup mayonnaise
2 tablespoons chopped fresh basil
4 large portobello mushrooms, stems removed
¼ teaspoon salt
¼ teaspoon black pepper
2 cloves garlic, minced
4 whole grain hamburger buns
4 ounces fresh mozzarella, cut into ¼-inch slices
2 jarred roasted red bell peppers, rinsed, patted dry and cut
　　into strips

1. Heat 1 teaspoon oil in medium saucepan over medium heat. Add shallots; cook 6 to 8 minutes or until golden brown and soft, stirring occasionally.

2. Combine mayonnaise and basil in small bowl; mix well.

3. Preheat broiler. Line baking sheet with foil. Drizzle both sides of mushrooms with remaining 2 teaspoons oil; season with salt and black pepper. Place mushrooms, cap side down, on prepared baking sheet; sprinkle with garlic.

4. Broil mushrooms 4 minutes per side or until tender.

5. Spread cut sides of buns with mayonnaise mixture. Layer shallots, mozzarella, mushrooms and roasted peppers on buns.

Makes 4 servings

Roasted Pepper Mushroom Burger

Curried Walnut Grain Burgers

    2 eggs
    ⅓ cup plain yogurt
    2 teaspoons curry powder
    2 teaspoons vegetarian Worcestershire sauce or soy sauce
    ½ teaspoon salt
    ¼ teaspoon ground red pepper
  1⅓ cups cooked couscous or brown rice
    ½ cup finely chopped walnuts
    ½ cup grated carrots
    ½ cup minced green onions
    ⅓ cup plain dry bread crumbs
    4 sesame seed hamburger buns
      Honey mustard
      Thinly sliced cucumber or apple

1. Lightly spray grid with nonstick cooking spray. Prepare grill for direct cooking.

2. Combine eggs, yogurt, curry powder, Worcestershire sauce, salt and red pepper in large bowl; beat until blended. Stir in couscous, walnuts, carrots, green onions and bread crumbs. Shape mixture into 4 patties about 1 inch thick.

3. Grill patties over medium-high heat 10 to 12 minutes until browned, turning once. Serve burgers on buns with mustard and cucumber.

Makes 4 servings

Note: Burgers can be also broiled 4 inches from heat source 5 to 6 minutes per side or until done.

Curried Walnut Grain Burger

Black Bean Burgers

2 cans (about 15 ounces each) black beans, rinsed and drained, divided
¾ cup plain dry bread crumbs
⅔ cup coarsely chopped green onions
2 egg whites
¼ cup chopped fresh basil
2 teaspoons onion powder
2 teaspoons dried oregano
1 teaspoon baking powder
1 teaspoon ground cumin
1 teaspoon black pepper
½ teaspoon salt
¾ cup corn
¾ cup chopped roasted red pepper
Nonstick cooking spray
6 whole wheat hamburger buns
Salsa
Avocado slices

1. Place half of beans, bread crumbs, green onions, egg whites, basil, onion powder, oregano, baking powder, cumin, black pepper and salt in food processor. Pulse 30 to 40 seconds or until mixture begins to hold together. Fold in remaining beans, corn and roasted red pepper. Let stand 20 minutes at room temperature.

2. Preheat oven to 350°F. Line baking sheet with parchment paper.

3. Shape mixture into 6 patties (about ½ cup each). Place patties on prepared baking sheet; spray tops with cooking spray.

4. Bake 18 to 20 minutes or until firm. Serve burgers on buns with salsa and avocado. *Makes 6 burgers*

Black Bean Burger

Middle Eastern Vegetable Grain Burgers

⅓ cup uncooked dried red lentils, sorted and rinsed
¼ cup uncooked brown or basmati rice
1 tablespoon olive oil
1 pound mushrooms, sliced
1 onion, chopped
¾ cup grated Parmesan cheese
½ cup walnuts, finely chopped
2 eggs
¼ cup chopped fresh cilantro
½ teaspoon black pepper
6 toasted sesame seed buns or toasted pita bread halves
  Mayonnaise
  Red onion slices
  Shredded lettuce
  Tomato slices

1. Place lentils in medium saucepan; cover with 1 inch water. Bring to a boil; reduce heat to low. Simmer, covered, 25 to 35 minutes or until tender. Rinse and drain; set aside. Meanwhile, cook rice according to package directions.

2. Heat oil in large heavy skillet over medium heat. Add mushrooms and chopped onion; cook and stir 20 to 25 minutes until mushrooms are brown. Combine mushroom mixture, cheese, walnuts, lentils, rice, eggs, cilantro and pepper in large bowl; mix well. Cover and chill.

3. Preheat broiler. Grease 15×10-inch jelly-roll pan with oil. Shape lentil mixture into 6 patties about ½ inch thick. Place patties on prepared pan.

4. Broil patties 4 inches from heat 6 to 8 minutes or until golden brown, turning once. Serve burgers on buns with mayonnaise, onion, lettuce and tomato. *Makes 6 servings*

Middle Eastern Vegetable Grain Burger

Beanie Burgers

  1 can (about 15 ounces) red kidney beans, rinsed and drained
  ½ cup chopped onion
  ⅓ cup quick oats
  1 egg
  1 tablespoon taco seasoning mix or mild chili powder
  ½ teaspoon salt
    Nonstick cooking spray
  4 slices cheese
  4 whole grain hamburger buns, split and toasted
    Lettuce leaves
    Tomato slices

1. Combine beans, onion, oats, egg, taco seasoning mix and salt in food processor. Pulse until blended and chunky, not smooth. (Mixture may be made up to 1 day in advance. Cover and refrigerate until needed.)

2. Spray large skillet with cooking spray; heat over medium heat. Shape bean mixture into 4 round patties.

3. Cook patties 4 minutes on one side; turn carefully with spatula. Top with cheese; cook 4 to 5 minutes.

4. Serve burgers on buns with lettuce and tomato.   *Makes 4 servings*

Beanie Burger

Chickpea Burgers

  1 can (15 ounces) chickpeas, rinsed and drained
⅓ cup chopped carrots
⅓ cup herbed croutons
¼ cup chopped fresh Italian parsley
¼ cup chopped onion
  1 egg white
  1 teaspoon minced garlic
  1 teaspoon grated lemon peel
½ teaspoon black pepper
⅛ teaspoon salt
    Nonstick cooking spray
  4 whole grain hamburger buns
    Tomato slices
    Lettuce leaves
    Salsa

1. Place chickpeas, carrots, croutons, parsley, onion, egg white, garlic, lemon peel, pepper and salt in food processor; process until blended. Shape mixture into 4 patties.

2. Spray large nonstick skillet with cooking spray; heat over medium heat. Cook patties 4 to 5 minutes or until bottoms are browned. Spray tops of patties with cooking spray; turn and cook 4 to 5 minutes or until browned.

3. Serve burgers on buns with tomato, lettuce and salsa.

Makes 4 servings

Chickpea Burger

Portabella Mushroom Burgers

REYNOLDS WRAP® Non-Stick Foil
3 tablespoons butter, melted
2 cloves garlic, minced
6 large portabella mushrooms
6 slices provolone cheese
6 hamburger buns

SAUCE
1 cup light sour cream
¼ cup Dijon mustard
2 tablespoons red wine vinegar
2 teaspoons sugar
⅛ teaspoon cayenne pepper

PREHEAT grill to medium-high. Make drainage holes in a sheet of Reynolds Wrap Non-Stick Foil with a large fork; set aside.

COMBINE butter and garlic. Baste mushroom caps with mixture. Place foil on grill grate with non-stick (dull) side facing up. Immediately place mushrooms on foil.

GRILL uncovered 6 to 8 minutes, turning once, until mushrooms are browned and tender. Place 1 slice of cheese on each mushroom during the last minute of grilling.

COMBINE sour cream, mustard, vinegar, sugar and pepper in small microwave-safe bowl to make sauce. Microwave on HIGH power 30 seconds or until warm. Serve sauce over burgers in buns.

Makes 6 servings

Prep Time: 15 minutes | Grill Time: 6 minutes

Portabella Mushroom Burger

Around the Globe

Stuffed Fiesta Burgers

1 pound ground beef
1 package (1¼ ounces) TACO BELL® HOME ORIGINALS®
    Taco Seasoning Mix
¼ cup PHILADELPHIA® Chive & Onion Cream Cheese Spread
⅓ cup KRAFT® Shredded Cheddar Cheese
4 hamburger buns, split, lightly toasted
½ cup TACO BELL® HOME ORIGINALS® Thick 'N Chunky
    Medium Salsa
1 avocado, peeled, pitted and cut into 8 slices

PREHEAT grill to medium heat. Mix meat and seasoning mix. Shape into 8 thin patties. Mix cream cheese spread and shredded cheese. Spoon about 2 tablespoons of the cheese mixture onto center of each of 4 of the patties; top with second patty. Pinch edges of patties together to seal.

GRILL 7 to 9 minutes on each side or until cooked through (160°F).

COVER bottom halves of buns with burgers. Top with salsa, avocados and top halves of buns.   *Makes 4 servings*

Prep Time: **15 minutes** | Grill Time: **9 minutes**

Mediterranean Burgers

1½ pounds ground beef
2 tablespoons grated Parmesan cheese
2 tablespoons chopped kalamata olives
1 tablespoon chopped fresh Italian parsley
1 tablespoon diced tomato
2 teaspoons dried oregano
1 teaspoon black pepper
4 slices mozzarella cheese
4 hamburger buns
   Lettuce leaves

1. Prepare grill for direct cooking.

2. Combine beef, Parmesan cheese, olives, parsley, tomato, oregano and pepper in medium bowl; mix lightly. Shape into 4 patties about ½ inch thick.

3. Grill patties, covered, over medium heat 8 to 10 minutes or until cooked through (160°F), turning once. Top burgers with mozzarella cheese during last minute of grilling.

4. Serve burgers on buns with lettuce.   *Makes 4 servings*

Serving Suggestion: For even more Mediterranean-inspired flavor, thinly slice bottled roasted red peppers and serve with burgers.

Mediterranean Burger

Curried Beef Burgers

    1 pound ground beef
    ¼ cup mango chutney, finely chopped
    ¼ cup grated apple
    1½ teaspoons curry powder
    ½ teaspoon salt
    ⅛ teaspoon black pepper
    1 large red onion, sliced ¼ inch thick
    4 Kaiser rolls or hamburger buns

1. Prepare grill for direct cooking. Combine beef, chutney, apple, curry powder, salt and pepper in medium bowl; mix lightly. Shape into 4 patties.

2. Grill patties, covered, over medium heat 8 to 10 minutes or until cooked through (160°F), turning once. Grill onion 5 minutes or until lightly charred, turning once. Serve burgers on rolls with onion.

Makes 4 servings

Classic Italian Burgers

    1½ pounds lean ground beef
    ¼ cup WISH-BONE® Italian Dressing
    ¼ cup finely chopped green onions
    2 tablespoons grated Parmesan cheese
    2 large cloves garlic, finely chopped
    4 hamburger buns
    4 slices mozzarella or provolone cheese (optional)
      Lettuce and tomato slices (optional)

In medium bowl, combine ground beef, Wish-Bone Italian Dressing, green onions, Parmesan and garlic; shape into four ¾-inch-thick patties. Grill 13 minutes or until desired doneness, turning once. Serve on buns with mozzarella cheese, lettuce and tomato.

Makes 4 servings

Curried Beef Burger

East Meets West Burgers

    1 pound ground beef (95% lean)
    ¼ cup soft whole wheat bread crumbs*
    1 large egg white
    ¼ teaspoon salt
    ⅛ teaspoon black pepper
    4 whole wheat hamburger buns, split

SESAME-SOY MAYONNAISE
    ¼ cup light mayonnaise
    1 tablespoon thinly sliced green onion, green part only
    ½ teaspoon soy sauce
    ¼ teaspoon dark sesame oil
    ⅛ teaspoon ground red pepper

SLAW TOPPING
    ½ cup romaine lettuce, thinly sliced
    ¼ cup shredded red cabbage
    ¼ cup shredded carrot
    1 teaspoon rice vinegar
    1 teaspoon vegetable oil
    ¼ teaspoon black pepper

To make soft bread crumbs, place torn bread in food processor or blender container. Cover; process, pulsing on and off, to form fine crumbs. One and one-half slices makes about 1 cup crumbs.

1. Combine Sesame-Soy Mayonnaise ingredients in small bowl; refrigerate until ready to use. Combine Slaw Topping ingredients in small bowl; set aside.

2. Combine ground beef, bread crumbs, egg white, salt and ⅛ teaspoon black pepper in large bowl, mixing lightly but thoroughly. Lightly shape into four ½-inch-thick patties.

3. Place patties on grid over medium ash-covered coals. Grill, covered, 11 to 13 minutes (over medium heat on preheated gas grill, covered, 7 to 8 minutes) until instant-read thermometer inserted horizontally into center registers 160°F, turning occasionally. About 2 minutes before burgers are done, place buns, cut sides down, on grid. Grill until lightly toasted.

continued on page 80

East Meets West Burger

4. Spread equal amount of Sesame-Soy Mayonnaise on bottom of each bun; top with burger. Evenly divide Slaw Topping over burgers. Close sandwiches.   *Makes 4 servings*

Prep and Cook Time: 30 to 40 minutes

Favorite recipe courtesy of *The Beef Checkoff*

Asian Turkey Burgers

      1 pound ground turkey
  1⅓ cups *French's®* French Fried Onions, divided
    ½ cup finely chopped water chestnuts
    ¼ cup dry bread crumbs
      1 egg
      3 tablespoons Asian stir-fry sauce or teriyaki baste & glaze sauce
      1 tablespoon *Frank's® RedHot®* Original Cayenne Pepper Sauce
      2 teaspoons grated fresh ginger *or* ½ teaspoon ground ginger
      4 sandwich buns
        Shredded lettuce

1. Combine turkey, *1 cup* French Fried Onions, water chestnuts, bread crumbs, egg, stir-fry sauce, *Frank's RedHot* Sauce and ginger in large bowl. Shape into 4 patties.

2. Broil patties 6 inches from heat, or grill over medium coals, 10 minutes or until no longer pink in center, turning once. Serve on buns. Top with remaining ⅓ *cup* onions and lettuce.

Makes 4 servings

Prep Time: 15 minutes | Cook Time: 10 minutes

Asian Turkey Burger

Greek Stuffed Burgers with Cucumber-Yogurt Sauce

1 (10-ounce) package frozen chopped spinach, thawed and
    squeezed dry
4 ounces (1 cup) feta cheese, crumbled
4 ounces (1 cup) sliced ripe olives
½ cup NEWMAN'S OWN® Balsamic Vinaigrette Salad Dressing
2 green onions, chopped
2 cloves garlic, minced
1 teaspoon dried oregano leaves
¾ teaspoon freshly ground black pepper, divided
1½ pounds lean ground beef
¼ teaspoon salt
    Cucumber-Yogurt Sauce (recipe follows)
4 whole wheat hamburger buns
    Lettuce leaves and tomato slices for garnish

With fork, mix spinach, feta cheese, olives, salad dressing, green onions, garlic, oregano and ½ teaspoon pepper. Set aside.

In medium bowl, mix ground beef with salt and remaining ¼ teaspoon pepper. Divide beef mixture into 8 equal portions; shape each into 3½-inch patty. Place heaping tablespoon of spinach mixture on 4 patties; top each with 1 remaining patty. Pinch edges of patties together to seal in spinach mixture.

Prepare Cucumber-Yogurt Sauce.

Lightly coat nonstick 12-inch skillet with olive oil spray. Heat skillet over medium heat; add burgers and cook 6 to 8 minutes, flipping halfway through cooking time, or until meat is cooked to desired doneness. Top burgers with remaining spinach mixture; cover skillet and cook 3 minutes. Serve burgers on buns garnished with lettuce, tomato and Cucumber-Yogurt Sauce. *Makes 4 servings*

Cucumber-Yogurt Sauce: In bowl, whisk together ½ cup plain low-fat yogurt, ½ small cucumber, peeled and finely chopped, and ¼ cup NEWMAN'S OWN® Balsamic Vinaigrette Salad Dressing.

Caribbean Beef Burgers with Mango Salsa

1 pound ground beef
2 teaspoons Caribbean jerk seasoning
  Salt

MANGO SALSA
1 large mango, peeled, coarsely chopped (about 1 cup)
1 tablespoon chopped fresh cilantro
1 tablespoon chopped green onion
1 tablespoon finely chopped seeded jalapeño pepper
1 tablespoon fresh lime juice

1. Combine ground beef and jerk seasoning in large bowl, mixing lightly but thoroughly. Shape into four ¾-inch-thick patties.

2. Place patties on grid over medium ash-covered coals. Grill, covered, 13 to 15 minutes (over medium heat on preheated gas grill, covered, 13 to 14 minutes) until instant-read thermometer inserted horizontally into center registers 160°F, turning occasionally. Season with salt, as desired.

3. Meanwhile, combine salsa ingredients in medium bowl, mixing lightly. Serve burgers with salsa. *Makes 4 servings*

Prep and Cook Time: **30 minutes**

Favorite recipe courtesy of *The Beef Checkoff*

> ■ **TIP:** Burgers may be served open-face on thick slices of Hawaiian or Challah bread, if desired. Toast bread on the grill.

Polynesian-Style Burgers

  1 pound ground beef
¼ cup chopped onion
¼ cup chopped green bell pepper
  3 teaspoons soy sauce, divided
½ teaspoon ground ginger, divided
¼ teaspoon garlic powder
  1 can (about 5 ounces) pineapple slices
  4 herbed hamburger buns
    Lettuce leaves

1. Prepare grill for direct cooking.

2. Combine beef, onion, bell pepper, 2 teaspoons soy sauce, ¼ teaspoon ginger and garlic powder; mix lightly. Shape into 4 patties.

3. Drain pineapple, reserving ¼ cup juice. Combine juice, remaining 1 teaspoon soy sauce and ¼ teaspoon ginger in pie plate. Add pineapple; turn to coat.

4. Grill patties, covered, over medium heat 8 to 10 minutes or until cooked through (160°F), turning once.

5. Grill pineapple until heated through. Serve burgers on buns with pineapple and lettuce.   *Makes 4 servings*

GRILLING

Polynesian-Style Burger

French Onion Burgers

1 pound ground beef
1 can (10½ ounces) CAMPBELL'S® Condensed French Onion Soup
4 slices Swiss cheese
4 round hard rolls, split

1. Shape the beef into 4 (½-inch-thick) burgers.

2. Heat a 10-inch skillet over medium-high heat. Add the burgers and cook until they're well browned on both sides. Remove the burgers from the skillet. Pour off any fat.

3. Stir the soup in the skillet and heat to a boil. Return the burgers to the skillet. Reduce the heat to low. Cover and cook for 5 minutes or until the burgers are cooked through. Top the burgers with the cheese and cook until the cheese is melted. Serve the burgers in the rolls with the soup mixture. *Makes 4 servings*

Kitchen Tip: You can also serve these burgers in a bowl atop a mound of hot mashed potatoes, with some of the onion gravy poured over.

Prep Time: **5 minutes** | Cook Time: **20 minutes**

CONTENTS

GREAT GRILLED BEEF

Tuscan Beef

  1 tablespoon olive oil
  2 cloves garlic, minced
1½ teaspoons dried rosemary, divided
  1 teaspoon salt
  ½ teaspoon black pepper
  4 beef ribeye or top loin (strip) steaks (¾ to 1 inch thick)
  ¾ cup tomato-basil or marinara pasta sauce
  ½ cup sliced pimiento-stuffed green olives
  1 tablespoon capers, drained

1. Prepare grill for direct cooking over medium-high heat. Combine oil, garlic, 1 teaspoon rosemary, salt and pepper in small bowl; mix well. Spread mixture evenly over both sides of steaks.

2. Grill steaks, covered, 4 to 5 minutes per side for medium-rare (145°F) or to desired doneness.

3. Meanwhile, combine pasta sauce, olives, capers and remaining ½ teaspoon rosemary in small saucepan; mix well. Cook and stir over medium heat until heated through. Serve steaks with sauce.

Makes 4 servings

Tuscan Beef

Szechuan Grilled Flank Steak

1 beef flank steak (1¼ to 1½ pounds)
¼ cup seasoned rice vinegar
¼ cup soy sauce
2 tablespoons dark sesame oil
4 cloves garlic, minced
2 teaspoons minced fresh ginger
½ teaspoon red pepper flakes
¼ cup water
½ cup thinly sliced green onions
2 to 3 teaspoons sesame seeds, toasted

1. Place steak in large resealable food storage bag. Combine vinegar, soy sauce, oil, garlic, ginger and red pepper flakes in small bowl; pour over steak. Press air from bag and seal; turn to coat. Marinate in refrigerator 3 hours, turning once.

2. Spray grid with nonstick cooking spray. Prepare grill for direct cooking. Drain steak, reserving marinade in small saucepan. Place steak on grid over medium heat. Grill, uncovered, 17 to 21 minutes for medium rare to medium or until desired doneness, turning once.

3. Add water to reserved marinade. Bring to a boil. Reduce heat; simmer 5 minutes. Transfer steak to carving board. Slice steak across grain into thin slices. Drizzle steak with boiled marinade. Sprinkle with green onions and sesame seeds.

Makes 4 to 6 servings

Hot Tip

For direct grilling, arrange hot coals in a single layer to extend 1 to 2 inches beyond the area of the food on the grid. This method is for quick-cooking foods, such as hamburgers, steaks, chicken breasts and fish.

Szechuan Grilled Flank Steak

Peppered Beef Ribeye Roast

1½ tablespoons black peppercorns
1 boneless beef ribeye roast (about 2½ to 3 pounds), well trimmed
¼ cup Dijon mustard
2 cloves garlic, minced
Sour Cream Sauce (recipe follows)

1. Prepare grill for indirect cooking.

2. Place peppercorns in small resealable food storage bag. Squeeze out excess air; close bag securely. Pound peppercorns using flat side of meat mallet or rolling pin until cracked. Set aside.

3. Pat roast dry with paper towels. Combine mustard and garlic in small bowl; spread over top and sides of roast. Sprinkle cracked pepper over mustard mixture.

4. Place roast, pepper-side up, on grid directly over drip pan. Grill, covered, over medium heat 1 hour to 1 hour 10 minutes for medium-rare to medium or until internal temperature reaches 135°F for medium-rare or 150°F for medium when tested with meat thermometer inserted into the thickest part of roast. Add 4 to 9 briquets to both sides of the fire after 45 minutes to maintain medium heat.

5. Meanwhile, prepare Sour Cream Sauce. Cover; refrigerate until serving.

6. Transfer roast to cutting board; cover with foil. Let stand 10 to 15 minutes before carving. Internal temperature will continue to rise 5°F to 10°F during stand time. Serve with Sour Cream Sauce.
Makes 6 to 8 servings

Sour Cream Sauce

¾ cup sour cream
2 tablespoons prepared horseradish
1 tablespoon balsamic vinegar
½ teaspoon sugar

Combine all ingredients in small bowl; mix well.
Makes about 1 cup

Peppered Beef Ribeye Roast

Beef Spiedini with Orzo

1/4 cup olive oil
1/4 cup dry red wine
 2 cloves garlic, minced
 1 teaspoon dried rosemary
1/2 teaspoon coarse salt
1/2 teaspoon dried thyme
1/2 teaspoon coarsely ground black pepper
1 1/2 pounds beef top sirloin steak, cut into 1×1 1/4-inch pieces
 6 cups water, plus additional for soaking
1/2 teaspoon salt
 1 cup uncooked orzo
 1 tablespoon butter
 1 tablespoon chopped parsley
   Fresh rosemary sprigs (optional)

1. Combine oil, wine, garlic, dried rosemary, coarse salt, thyme and pepper in large resealable food storage bag. Add beef; turn to coat. Marinate in refrigerator 15 to 30 minutes.

2. Prepare grill for direct cooking. Soak 8 (6- to 8-inch) wooden skewers in water 15 minutes.

3. Bring 6 cups water and salt to a boil in small saucepan over high heat. Add orzo; reduce heat and simmer 15 minutes or until tender. Drain. Stir in butter and parsley; keep warm.

4. Thread beef onto skewers. Grill over medium-high heat 8 to 10 minutes, turning occasionally. Serve with orzo. Garnish skewers with fresh rosemary.

Makes 4 serving

Beef Spiedini with Orzo

Honey Mustard Steaks with Grilled Onions

4 boneless beef top loin (strip) steaks, cut 1 inch thick
⅓ cup coarse-grain Dijon-style mustard
1 tablespoon plus 1½ teaspoons honey
1 tablespoon chopped parsley
1 tablespoon cider vinegar
1 tablespoon water
¼ teaspoon hot pepper sauce
⅛ teaspoon coarse grind black pepper
1 large red onion, sliced ½ inch thick

Combine mustard, honey, parsley, vinegar, water, hot pepper sauce and pepper.
Place beef steaks and onion slices on grid over medium coals; brush both with
mustard mixture. Grill 9 to 12 minutes for rare (140°F) to medium (160°F), turning
once and brushing with mustard mixture. *Makes 4 servings*

Prep Time: 30 minutes

Favorite recipe from **North Dakota Beef Commission**

Hot Tip

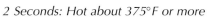

To check the temperature of the coals, cautiously
hold the palm of your hand at grid level—over the
coals for direct heat and over the drip pan for
indirect heat. Count the number of seconds you can
hold your hand in that position before the heat
forces you to pull it away.

2 Seconds: Hot about 375°F or more

3 Seconds: Medium-hot about 350°F to 375°F

4 Seconds: Medium about 300°F to 350°F

5 Seconds: Low about 200°F to 300°F

Honey Mustard Steaks with Grilled Onions

Peppered Steak with Dijon Sauce

4 boneless beef top loin (New York strip) steaks, cut 1 inch thick
    (about 1½ pounds)
1 tablespoon *French's®* Worcestershire Sauce
  Crushed black pepper
⅓ cup mayonnaise
⅓ cup *French's®* Honey Dijon Mustard
3 tablespoons dry red wine
2 tablespoons minced red or green onion
2 tablespoons minced fresh parsley
1 clove garlic, minced

1. Brush steaks with Worcestershire and sprinkle with pepper to taste; set aside. To prepare Dijon sauce, combine mayonnaise, mustard, wine, onion, parsley and garlic in medium bowl.

2. Place steaks on grid. Grill steaks over high heat 15 minutes for medium rare or to desired doneness, turning often. Serve with Dijon sauce. Garnish as desired.

Makes 4 serving.

Serving Suggestion: Dijon sauce is also great served with grilled salmon and swordfish. To serve with fish, substitute white wine for red wine and minced fresh dil for fresh parsley.

Prep Time: 10 minutes
Cook Time: 15 minutes

Hot Tip

Use long-handled tongs or a spatula to turn meat. A fork or knife punctures the meat and lets the juices escape.

Peppered Steak with Dijon Sauce

Grilled Italian Steak

1 cup WISH-BONE® Italian Dressing*
3 tablespoons grated Parmesan cheese
3 teaspoons dried basil leaves, crushed
¼ teaspoon cracked black pepper
1 (2- to 3-pound) boneless sirloin or top round steak

*Also terrific with WISH-BONE® Robusto Italian Dressing.

In small bowl, combine all ingredients except steak. Add steak; turn to coat. Cover or close bag and marinate in refrigerator, turning occasionally, 3 to 24 hours.

In nonaluminum baking dish or plastic bag, pour ¾ cup marinade over steak. Cover or close bag and marinate in refrigerator, turning occasionally, 3 to 24 hours. Refrigerate remaining marinade.

Remove steak from marinade, discarding marinade. Grill or broil steak, turning once and brushing frequently with reserved marinade, until steak is desired doneness.

Makes 8 servings

Hot Tip

Watch foods carefully during grilling. Total cooking time will vary with the type of food, position on the grill, temperature of the coals, weather and degree of doneness you desire.

Mexican Steak with Chimichurri Sauce

⅔ cup olive oil
½ cup minced fresh parsley
⅓ cup *Frank's® RedHot®* Original Cayenne Pepper Sauce
3 tablespoons lime juice
1 tablespoon *French's®* Worcestershire Sauce
2 teaspoons dried oregano leaves
2 cloves garlic, minced
2 pounds boneless beef sirloin (1½ inches thick)

Place oil, parsley, **Frank's RedHot** Sauce, lime juice, Worcestershire, oregano and garlic in blender or food processor. Cover and process until well blended. Reserve ⅔ cup sauce mixture. Place steak in large resealable food storage bag. Pour remaining sauce mixture over steak. Seal bag and marinate in refrigerator 30 minutes.

Place steak on grid, discarding marinade. Grill over hot coals 10 minutes per side for medium-rare or to desired doneness. Let steak stand 5 minutes. Slice steak diagonally. Serve with reserved sauce mixture.   *Makes 6 to 8 servings*

Prep Time: 10 minutes
Marinate Time: 30 minutes
Cook Time: 20 minutes

Korean Beef Short Ribs

2½ pounds beef chuck flanken-style short ribs, cut ⅜ to ½ inch thick*
 ¼ cup chopped green onions
 ¼ cup water
 ¼ cup soy sauce
 1 tablespoon sugar
 2 teaspoons grated fresh ginger
 2 cloves garlic, minced
 2 teaspoons dark sesame oil
 ½ teaspoon black pepper
 1 tablespoon sesame seeds, toasted

*Flanken-style ribs can be ordered from your butcher. They are cross-cut short ribs sawed through the bones, ⅜ to ½ inch thick.

1. Place ribs in large resealable food storage bag. Combine green onions, water, soy sauce, sugar, ginger, garlic, oil and pepper in small bowl; pour over ribs. Seal bag tightly, turning to coat. Marinate in refrigerator 4 to 24 hours, turning occasionally.

2. Spray grid with nonstick cooking spray. Prepare grill for direct cooking.

3. Drain ribs; reserve marinade. Place ribs on grid. Grill ribs, covered, over medium-hot coals 5 minutes. Brush tops lightly with reserved marinade; turn and brush again. Discard remaining marinade. Continue to grill, covered, 5 to 6 minutes for medium or until desired doneness is reached. Sprinkle with sesame seeds.

Makes 4 to 6 servings

Hot Tip

For food safety, allow the meat or poultry to cook on the grill at least 5 minutes after the last application of marinade or sauce. If using leftover marinade for a sauce with cooked food, boil it at least 1 minute.

Korean Beef Short Ribs

Texas Meets N.Y. Strip Steaks

3 tablespoons olive oil, divided
2 medium onions, thinly sliced)
4 strip steaks (6 to 8 ounces each)
2 teaspoons minced garlic
2 teaspoons cracked black pepper

1. Heat 2 tablespoons oil in medium skillet over medium heat. Add onions; cook and stir 15 to 20 minutes or until soft and golden brown.

2. Meanwhile, prepare grill for direct cooking. Rub steaks with remaining 1 tablespoon oil and garlic. Sprinkle pepper on both sides of steaks.

3. Grill steaks over medium-high heat 10 to 12 minutes to at least 145°F or until desired doneness, turning twice to obtain cross-hatch grill marks. Serve steaks topped with onions.   *Makes 4 servings*

Beef and Pineapple Kabobs

1 boneless beef top sirloin or top round steak (about 1 pound)
1 small onion, finely chopped
½ cup teriyaki sauce
16 pieces (1-inch cubes) fresh pineapple
1 can (8 ounces) water chestnuts, drained

1. Cut steak into ¼-inch-thick strips. Combine onion and teriyaki sauce in small bowl. Add beef strips, stirring to coat.

2. Prepare grill for direct cooking. If using bamboo skewers, soak in water for 20 to 30 minutes before using, to prevent them from burning.

3. Alternately thread beef strips (weaving back and forth), pineapple and water chestnuts onto skewers.

4. Place kabobs on grid over medium heat. Grill 4 minutes, turning once, or until meat is cooked through. Serve immediately.   *Makes 4 servings*

Note: Recipe can also be prepared with flank steak.

Serving Suggestion: Serve with hot cooked rice and stir-fried broccoli, mushrooms and red bell peppers.

Texas Meets N.Y. Strip Steak

Rib Eye Steaks with Chili Butter

½ cup (1 stick) butter, softened
2 teaspoons chili powder
1 teaspoon minced garlic
1 teaspoon Dijon mustard
⅛ teaspoon ground red pepper or chipotle chile pepper
4 beef rib eye steaks
1 teaspoon black pepper

1. Beat butter, chili powder, garlic, mustard and red pepper in medium bowl until smooth.

2. Place mixture on sheet of waxed paper. Roll mixture back and forth into 6-inch log using waxed paper. If butter is too soft, refrigerate up to 30 minutes. Wrap with waxed paper; refrigerate at least 1 hour or up to 2 days.

3. Prepare grill for direct cooking. Rub black pepper evenly over both sides of steaks.

4. Place steaks on grid over medium-high heat. Grill, covered, 8 to 10 minutes or until desired doneness, turning occasionally. Serve with slices of Chili Butter.

Makes 4 serving

Rib Eye Steak with Chili Butter

Steak Provençal

4 beef sirloin, tenderloin or ribeye steaks (about 11 ounces each)
5 tablespoons I CAN'T BELIEVE IT'S NOT BUTTER!® Spread
2 large cloves garlic, finely chopped
1½ cups chopped tomatoes (about 2 medium)
1 to 2 tablespoons rinsed and chopped large capers
¼ teaspoon salt
¼ teaspoon ground black pepper
2 tablespoons chopped fresh parsley

Grill or broil steaks to desired doneness.

Meanwhile, in 10-inch skillet, melt I Can't Believe It's Not Butter!® Spread and cook garlic over medium heat, stirring occasionally, 30 seconds. Add tomatoes, capers, salt and pepper. Cook, stirring occasionally, 3 minutes or until tomatoes are cooked and mixture is saucy. Stir in parsley. Serve over hot steaks.   *Makes 4 serving*

Hot Tip

Capers are the flower buds of a Mediterranean bush. They are usually sold in jars pickled in brine. Capers should be rinsed in a colander before using to make them less salty.

Steak Provençal

Bold and Zesty Beef Back Ribs

5 pounds beef back ribs, cut into 3- or 4-rib pieces
Salt and black pepper
1 teaspoon vegetable oil
1 small onion, minced
2 cloves garlic, minced
1 cup ketchup
½ cup chili sauce
2 tablespoons lemon juice
1 tablespoon packed brown sugar
1 teaspoon hot pepper sauce

1. Place ribs in shallow pan; season with salt and black pepper. Refrigerate until ready to grill.

2. Prepare grill for indirect cooking.

3. Meanwhile, heat oil in large nonstick saucepan over medium heat. Add onion and garlic; cook and stir 5 minutes or until onion is tender. Stir in ketchup, chili sauce, lemon juice, brown sugar and hot pepper sauce. Reduce heat to medium-low. Cook 15 minutes, stirring occasionally.

4. Place ribs on grid directly over drip pan. Baste ribs generously with sauce. Grill, covered, 45 to 60 minutes or until ribs are tender and browned, turning occasionally.

5. Bring remaining sauce to a boil over medium-high heat; boil 1 minute. Serve ribs with sauce. *Makes 5 to 6 servings*

Prep Time: 15 minutes
Cook Time: 1 hour 5 minutes to 1 hour 20 minutes

Bold and Zesty Beef Back Ribs

Greek-Style Steak Sandwiches

2 teaspoons Greek seasoning or dried oregano
1 beef flank steak (about 1½ pounds)
4 rounds pita bread, sliced in half crosswise
½ cup sliced red onion
1 small cucumber, thinly sliced
½ cup chopped tomato
½ cup crumbled feta cheese
¼ cup red wine vinaigrette
1 cup plain yogurt

1. Press Greek seasoning into both sides of steak. Place steak in large resealable food storage bag. Seal bag; turn to coat. Marinate in refrigerator 30 to 60 minutes.

2. Prepare grill for direct cooking.

3. Place steak on grid over medium-high heat. Grill, covered, 17 to 21 minutes or until desired doneness, turning once. Transfer steak to cutting board; let stand, covered with tented foil, 10 minutes before slicing.

4. Meanwhile, grill pitas about 1 minute on both sides or until warm. Slice steak across grain into thin strips.

5. Divide meat evenly among pitas. Top each with onion, cucumber, tomato and feta cheese. Drizzle 1½ teaspoons vinaigrette over each pita; top with 1 to 2 tablespoons yogurt. *Makes 8 sandwiches*

Greek-Style Steak Sandwiches

Ginger Beef and Carrot Kabobs

1 boneless beef top sirloin steak (¾ pound, 1 inch thick), cut into 1-inch cubes
¼ cup reduced-sodium soy sauce
3 tablespoons water, divided
1 tablespoon honey
1 teaspoon olive oil
1 clove garlic, minced
¼ teaspoon ground ginger
¼ teaspoon ground allspice
⅛ teaspoon ground red pepper
2 medium carrots, cut into 1-inch pieces (about 1½ cups)
4 green onions, trimmed to 4-inch pieces

1. Place beef in large resealable food storage bag. Combine soy sauce, 1 tablespoon water, honey, olive oil, garlic, ginger, allspice and red pepper in small bowl. Pour over meat in bag. Seal bag; turn to coat meat. Marinate in refrigerator 4 to 16 hours, turning bag occasionally.

2. Meanwhile, place remaining 2 tablespoons water in medium saucepan. Bring water to a boil. Add carrots. Cover; cook 5 minutes or until crisp-tender. Drain.

3. Prepare grill for direct cooking. Spray grid with nonstick cooking spray. Drain meat. Discard marinade. Alternately thread meat and carrot pieces onto 4 skewers. Add green onion piece to end of each skewer.

4. Grill kabobs over medium coals 11 to 14 minutes or until meat is tender, turning once during grilling. *Makes 4 serving.*

Prep Time: 10 minutes
Marinate Time: 4 to 16 hours
Grill Time: 11 to 14 minutes

Ginger Beef and Carrot Kabobs

Barbecued Pork & Lamb

Cuban Garlic & Lime Pork Chops

6 boneless pork top loin chops, ¾ inch thick (about 1½ pounds)
2 tablespoons olive oil
2 tablespoons lime juice
2 tablespoons orange juice
2 teaspoons minced garlic
½ teaspoon salt, divided
½ teaspoon red pepper flakes
2 small seedless oranges, peeled and chopped
1 medium cucumber, peeled, seeded and chopped
2 tablespoons chopped onion
2 tablespoons chopped fresh cilantro

1. Place pork in large resealable food storage bag. Add oil, juices, garlic, ¼ teaspoon salt and pepper flakes. Seal bag and shake to evenly distribute marinade; refrigerate up to 24 hours.

2. Combine oranges, cucumber, onion and cilantro in small bowl; toss lightly. Cover and refrigerate 1 hour or overnight. Add remaining ¼ teaspoon salt just before serving.

3. Spray grid with nonstick cooking spray. Prepare grill for indirect cooking. Remove pork from marinade; discard marinade. Grill or broil pork 6 to 8 minutes on each side or until desired doneness. Serve with orange mixture.   *Makes 6 servings*

Make-Ahead Time: 1 day before cooking
Final Prep and Cook Time: 16 minutes

Cuban Garlic & Lime Pork Chops

Tangy Barbecued Lamb

¾ cup prepared chili sauce
½ cup honey
½ cup beer (not light beer)
¼ cup reduced-sodium Worcestershire sauce
¼ cup finely chopped onion
2 cloves garlic, minced
½ teaspoon red pepper flakes
¼ teaspoon sea salt
5 pounds lamb ribs, well trimmed, cut into individual ribs

1. Combine chili sauce, honey, beer, Worcestershire sauce, onion, garlic, pepper flakes and salt in small saucepan; bring to a boil. Reduce heat; simmer, covered, 10 minutes. Remove from heat; cool to room temperature.

2. Place lamb in large resealable food storage bag; add chili mixture. Seal bag tightly; turn to coat. Marinate in refrigerator at least 2 hours, turning occasionally.

3. Rub oil over grid to prevent sticking. Prepare grill for indirect cooking over medium heat.

4. Remove lamb from marinade; reserve marinade. Arrange lamb on grid over drip pan. Cover; cook 15 minutes. Turn lamb and brush with marinade. Cover; cook 15 minutes. Turn lamb and brush with marinade again. Cover; cook 15 minutes longer or until meat is tender. Place remaining marinade in small saucepan and bring to a boil; boil 1 minute. Serve with lamb.   *Makes 6 servings*

Note: To set up gas grill for indirect cooking, preheat all burners on high. Turn one burner off; place food over "off" burner. Reset remaining burner(s) to medium. Close lid to cook. To set up charcoal grill for indirect cooking, arrange hot coals around outer edge of grill; place disposable aluminum pan in open space. Place food over open area and close lid to cook.

Tangy Barbecued Lamb

Marinated Italian Sausage and Peppers

½ cup olive oil
¼ cup red wine vinegar
2 tablespoons chopped fresh parsley
1 tablespoon dried oregano leaves
2 cloves garlic, crushed
1 teaspoon salt
1 teaspoon black pepper
4 hot or sweet Italian sausage links
1 large onion, sliced into rings
1 large bell pepper, quartered
Horseradish-Mustard Spread (recipe follows)

1. Combine oil, vinegar, parsley, oregano, garlic, salt and black pepper in small bowl. Place sausages, onion and bell pepper in large resealable food storage bag; pour marinade into bag. Seal bag; turn to coat. Marinate in refrigerator 1 to 2 hours.

2. Prepare Horseradish-Mustard Spread; set aside. Spray grid with nonstick cooking spray. Prepare grill for direct cooking. Drain sausages, onion and bell pepper; reserve marinade.

3. Grill sausages, covered, 4 to 5 minutes. Turn sausages and place onion and bell pepper on grid. Brush sausages and vegetables with reserved marinade. Grill, covered, 5 minutes or until vegetables are crisp-tender, turning vegetables halfway through grilling time. Serve sausages, onions and bell peppers with Horseradish-Mustard Spread. *Makes 4 servings*

Horseradish-Mustard Spread

3 tablespoons mayonnaise
1 tablespoon chopped fresh parsley
1 tablespoon prepared horseradish
1 tablespoon Dijon mustard
2 teaspoons garlic powder
1 teaspoon black pepper

Combine all ingredients in small bowl; mix well. *Makes about ½ cup*

Marinated Italian Sausage and Peppers

Ginger Peanut Pork Tenderloin

3 tablespoons soy sauce
1 tablespoon honey
1 tablespoon dark sesame oil
1 tablespoon creamy peanut butter
1 tablespoon minced fresh ginger
2 teaspoons TABASCO® brand Pepper Sauce
1 large clove garlic, minced
1 teaspoon curry powder
½ teaspoon salt
1½ pounds pork tenderloins

Combine all ingredients except pork in medium bowl. Set aside 2 tablespoons mixture. Add pork tenderloins to bowl; cover and marinate at least 2 hours or overnight, turning occasionally.

Preheat grill to medium, placing rack 5 to 6 inches above coals. Place tenderloins on rack; grill 20 to 25 minutes or until no longer pink in center, turning occasionally and brushing frequently with marinade during first 10 minutes of grilling. Let stand 10 minutes before slicing. Brush reserved 2 tablespoons soy sauce mixture over cooked meat. *Makes 6 servings*

Coriander-Pepper Chops

4 boneless pork chops, 1-inch thick
3 tablespoons low-sodium soy sauce
1 tablespoon crushed coriander seeds
1 tablespoon brown sugar
1 tablespoon coarsely ground black pepper
2 cloves garlic, crushed

Combine all ingredients except pork chops. Place chops in a shallow dish and pour marinade over; let marinate 30 minutes. Spray grid with nonstick cooking spray. Prepare grill for direct cooking. Remove pork from marinade; discard marinade and grill chops for 7 to 8 minutes, turning once. Or broil chops 3 to 4 inches from heat source 7 to 8 minutes, turning once. Cook until meat thermometer reads 160°F. *Makes 4 servings*

*Favorite recipe from **National Pork Board***

Ginger Peanut Pork Tenderloin

Marinated Grilled Lamb Chops

8 well-trimmed lamb loin chops, 1 inch thick (about 2¼ pounds)
3 cloves garlic, minced
2 tablespoons chopped fresh rosemary *or* 2 teaspoons dried rosemary
2 tablespoons chopped fresh mint *or* 2 teaspoons dried mint
¾ cup dry red wine
⅓ cup butter or margarine, softened
¼ teaspoon salt
¼ teaspoon black pepper
Fresh mint leaves (optional)

1. Place chops in large resealable food storage bag. Combine garlic, rosemary and min in small bowl. Combine half of garlic mixture and wine in small bowl. Pour wine mixtur over chops in bag. Seal bag; turn to coat. Marinate in refrigerator at least 2 hours or u to 4 hours, turning occasionally.

2. Add butter, salt and pepper to remaining garlic mixture; mix well. Spoon onto center of sheet of plastic wrap. Shape butter mixture into 4×1½-inch log using plastic wrap. Wrap securely; refrigerate until ready to serve.

3. Spray grid with nonstick cooking spray. Prepare grill for direct cooking. Drain chops, discarding marinade. Place chops on grid. Grill, covered, over medium coals about 9 minutes or until instant-read thermometer inserted into chops registers 160°F for medium or to desired doneness, turning once.

4. Cut butter log crosswise into 8 (½-inch) slices. To serve, top each chop with slice o seasoned butter. Garnish with mint leaves, if desired.   *Makes 4 serving*

Hot Tip

Prevent food from sticking to the grill by keeping the grill rack clean. Start by cleaning the rack with a wire brush before heating. Preheating the rack at least 15 minutes before starting to cook also keeps food from sticking. However, brushing the rack after cooking is the best way to keep the rack clean.

Marinated Grilled Lamb Chops

Tex-Mex Pork Kabobs
with Chili Sour Cream Sauce

2¼ teaspoons chili powder, divided
1¾ teaspoons cumin, divided
¾ teaspoon garlic powder, divided
¾ teaspoon onion powder, divided
¾ teaspoon dried oregano, divided
1 pork tenderloin (1½ pounds), trimmed and cut into 1-inch pieces
1 cup reduced-fat sour cream
¾ teaspoon salt, divided
¼ teaspoon black pepper
1 large red bell pepper, cored, seeded and cut into small chunks
1 large green bell pepper, cored, seeded and cut into small chunks
1 large yellow bell pepper, cored, seeded and cut into small chunks

1. Blend 1½ teaspoons chili powder, 1 teaspoon cumin, ½ teaspoon garlic powder, ½ teaspoon onion powder and ½ teaspoon oregano in medium bowl. Add pork. Toss well to coat. Cover tightly; refrigerate 2 to 3 hours.

2. Combine sour cream, remaining ¾ teaspoon chili powder, ¾ teaspoon cumin, ¼ teaspoon garlic powder, ¼ teaspoon onion powder, ¼ teaspoon oregano, ¼ teaspoon salt and black pepper in small bowl. Mix well. Cover tightly and refrigerate 2 to 3 hours.

3. If using wooden skewers, soak in water 20 minutes before using. Spray grid with nonstick cooking spray. Prepare grill or broiler for direct cooking.

4. Toss pork with remaining ½ teaspoon salt. Thread meat and peppers onto skewers. Grill over medium-hot coals 10 minutes or until desired doneness, turning several times. If broiling, place kabobs on foil-lined baking sheet. Broil 8 inches from heat 5 minutes per side or until desired doneness, turning once. Serve immediately with Chili Sour Cream Sauce. *Makes 4 to 6 servings*

Tex-Mex Pork Kabobs with Chili Sour Cream Sauce

Calypso Pork Chops

  1 teaspoon paprika
  ½ teaspoon dried thyme
  ¼ teaspoon salt
  ¼ teaspoon ground allspice
  4 center-cut pork loin chops (about 1½ pounds), cut ¾ inch thick
  5 tablespoons fresh lime juice, divided
  2 tablespoons plus 1½ teaspoons seeded, chopped jalapeño peppers,* divided
  1 tablespoon vegetable oil
1½ teaspoons grated fresh ginger, divided
  1 teaspoon sugar
  1 ripe medium papaya, peeled, seeded and chopped (about 1½ cups)
  ¼ cup finely diced red bell pepper
     Additional chopped jalapeño pepper (optional)

*Jalapeño peppers can sting and irritate the skin; wear rubber gloves when handling peppers and do not touch eyes. Wash hands after handling.

1. Combine paprika, thyme, salt and allspice in small bowl; rub over both sides of pork chops. Place chops in large resealable food storage bag.

2. Combine 3 tablespoons lime juice, 2 tablespoons jalapeño, oil, 1 teaspoon ginger and sugar in small bowl; pour over chops. Seal bag; turn to coat. Marinate in refrigerator 1 to 2 hours.

3. Combine papaya, bell pepper, remaining 2 tablespoons lime juice, remaining 1½ teaspoons jalapeño and remaining ½ teaspoon ginger in another small bowl; cover and refrigerate until serving.

4. Spray grid with nonstick cooking spray. Prepare grill for direct cooking.

5. Drain chops; discard marinade. Grill chops, covered, over medium coals 10 to 12 minutes or until meat thermometer inserted into center reads 155°F for medium or until desired doneness, turning halfway through grilling time. Top chops with papaya mixture. Garnish with peppers, if desired. *Makes 4 serving*

Calypso Pork Chop

Balsamic Spiced Lamb Kabobs

1 pound boneless American lamb (leg or shoulder), cut into 1¼-inch cubes
3 tablespoons balsamic vinegar or red wine vinegar
2 tablespoons water
2 tablespoons olive oil
2 cloves garlic, minced
1 teaspoon dried rosemary leaves
½ teaspoon salt
½ teaspoon ground cumin
¼ teaspoon ground coriander
¼ teaspoon ground red pepper
¼ teaspoon black pepper
½ firm cantaloupe, peeled and cut into 1- to 2-inch pieces
16 green onions, cut into 2- to 3-inch pieces

Place lamb in heavy-duty resealable food storage bag set in shallow dish. For marinade, in medium bowl combine vinegar, water, oil, garlic, rosemary, salt, cumin coriander, red pepper and black pepper. Pour marinade over lamb in bag. Seal bag; turn to coat. Marinate in refrigerator 6 to 8 hours, stirring occasionally. Drain lamb, reserving marinade.

Thread lamb, cantaloupe and green onions on four 14-inch skewers. Brush with marinade. Place on grill rack directly over medium coals. Grill 4 inches from coals 15 to 20 minutes or to desired doneness, turning once and brushing with marinade. (Or, broil 3 to 4 inches from heat 10 to 15 minutes, turning once and brushing with marinade.) *Makes 4 serving*

Prep Time: 15 minutes
Marinating Time: 6 to 8 hours
Cook Time: 15 to 20 minutes

Favorite recipe from **American Lamb Council**

Herb Butterflied Leg of Lamb

1 (6- to 8-pound) leg of American lamb, boned and butterflied*
⅓ cup olive oil
⅓ cup lemon juice
¼ cup dry sherry (optional)
¼ cup water
2 tablespoons finely chopped shallots or green onion
1 tablespoon chopped fresh oregano
1 tablespoon chopped fresh rosemary

*Have butcher bone leg of lamb, then slit leg lengthwise and spread flat.

Trim fat from lamb. For marinade, in small bowl combine oil, lemon juice, sherry, if desired, water, shallots, oregano and rosemary. Place lamb in large shallow baking dish; pour marinade over lamb. Cover and marinate in refrigerator 8 hours or overnight, turning occasionally. Drain lamb, reserving marinade.

Place lamb on grill rack directly over medium coals. Grill 4 inches from coals 40 to 50 minutes or to desired doneness, turning every 15 minutes and brushing with marinade. (Or, broil 4 to 5 inches from heat 50 to 65 minutes, turning every 15 minutes and brushing with marinade.)   *Makes 24 servings*

Prep Time: 10 minutes
Marinating Time: 8 hours or overnight
Cook Time: 40 to 50 minutes

*Favorite recipe from **American Lamb Council***

Jerk Ribs

2 pounds pork back ribs
2 tablespoons dried minced onion
4 teaspoons ground thyme
1 tablespoon sugar
1 tablespoon onion powder
2 teaspoons salt
2 teaspoons ground allspice
2 teaspoons black pepper
1 teaspoon ground red pepper
1/2 teaspoon ground nutmeg
1/2 teaspoon ground cinnamon

Place all ingredients except ribs in small jar with tight-fitting lid; cover and shake until well blended. Rub dry mixture onto all surfaces of ribs.

Prepare grill with rectangular foil drip pan. Bank briquets on either side of drip pan for indirect cooking. Place ribs on grid over drip pan. Grill, on covered grill, over low coals 1 1/2 hours or until ribs are tender, turning occasionally. To serve, cut into 1- or 2-rib portions. *Makes 10 servings*

Conventional Directions: Prepare rub as directed. Roast ribs on rack in shallow pan in 350°F oven for 1 1/2 hours or until ribs are tender.

Prep Time: 10 minutes
Cook Time: 90 minutes

Favorite recipe from **National Pork Board**

Jerk Ribs

HOT-OFF-THE-GRILL POULTRY

Chicken Tikka (Tandoori-Style Grilled Chicken)

2 chickens (3 pounds each), cut up
1 pint nonfat yogurt
½ cup *Frank's® RedHot®* Original Cayenne Pepper Sauce
1 tablespoon grated peeled fresh ginger
3 cloves garlic, minced
1 tablespoon paprika
1 tablespoon cumin seeds, crushed *or* 1½ teaspoons ground cumin
2 teaspoons salt
1 teaspoon ground coriander

Remove skin and visible fat from chicken pieces. Rinse with cold water and pat dry. Randomly poke chicken all over with tip of sharp knife. Place chicken in resealable food storage bags or large glass bowl. Combine yogurt, **Frank's RedHot** Sauce, ginger, garlic, paprika, cumin, salt and coriander in small bowl; mix well. Pour over chicken pieces, turning pieces to coat evenly. Seal bags or cover bowl and marinate in refrigerator 1 hour or overnight.

Place chicken on oiled grid, reserving marinade. Grill over medium coals 45 minutes or until chicken is no longer pink near bone and juices run clear, turning and basting often with marinade. (Do not baste during last 10 minutes of cooking.) Discard any remaining marinade. Serve warm. *Makes 6 to 8 servings*

Prep Time: 15 minutes
Marinate Time: 1 hour
Cook Time: 45 minutes

Chicken Tikka (Tandoori-Style Grilled Chicken)

Grilled Lemon Chicken Dijon

⅓ cup HOLLAND HOUSE® White with Lemon Cooking Wine
⅓ cup olive oil
2 tablespoons Dijon mustard
1 teaspoon dried thyme leaves
2 whole chicken breasts, skinned, boned and halved

In shallow baking dish combine cooking wine, oil, mustard and thyme. Add chicken and turn to coat. Cover; marinate in refrigerator for 1 to 2 hours.

Prepare grill for direct cooking. Drain chicken, reserving marinade. Grill chicken over medium coals 12 to 16 minutes or until cooked through, turning once and basting with marinade.*   *Makes 4 servings*

*Do not baste during last 5 minutes of grilling.

Reuben Chicken Melts

4 boneless skinless chicken breast halves
1 large onion, cut into ½-inch slices
1¼ cups Thousand Island salad dressing, divided
2 cups shredded red cabbage
1½ cups (6 ounces) shredded Swiss cheese
4 French rolls, split

1. Prepare grill for direct cooking.

2. Brush chicken and onion with ½ cup salad dressing.

2. Combine ¼ cup salad dressing and cabbage; mix well. Set aside.

3. Grill chicken over high heat 5 to 7 minutes per side or until no longer pink in center. Sprinkle chicken evenly with cheese during last minute of grilling. Grill onion 4 to 5 minutes per side or until browned and tender. Grill rolls until toasted.

4. Spread toasted sides of rolls with remaining ½ cup salad dressing. Place chicken on bottoms of rolls. Top with onion, cabbage mixture and tops of rolls. Serve immediately.   *Makes 4 servings*

Prep and Cook Time: 25 minutes

Grilled Lemon Chicken Dijon

Grilled Chicken Tostadas

    1 pound boneless skinless chicken breasts
    1 teaspoon ground cumin
    ¼ cup orange juice
    ¼ cup plus 2 tablespoons salsa, divided
    1 tablespoon plus 2 teaspoons vegetable oil, divided
    2 cloves garlic, minced
    8 green onions
    1 can (16 ounces) refried beans
    4 (10-inch) flour tortillas
    2 cups chopped romaine lettuce
 1½ cups (6 ounces) shredded Monterey Jack cheese with jalapeño peppers
    1 ripe medium avocado, diced
    1 medium tomato, seeded and diced
      Chopped fresh cilantro and sour cream (optional)

1. Place chicken in single layer in shallow glass dish; sprinkle with cumin. Combine orange juice, ¼ cup salsa, 1 tablespoon oil and garlic in small bowl; pour over chicken. Cover; marinate in refrigerator at least 2 hours or up to 8 hours, stirring mixture occasionally.

2. Prepare grill for direct cooking.

3. Drain chicken; reserve marinade. Brush green onions with remaining 2 teaspoons oil. Place chicken and green onions on grid. Grill, covered, over medium-high heat 5 minutes. Brush tops of chicken with half of reserved marinade; turn and brush with remaining marinade. Turn onions. Continue to grill, covered, 5 minutes or until chicken is no longer pink in center and onions are tender. (Remove onions as soon as they are done.)

4. Meanwhile, combine beans and remaining 2 tablespoons salsa in small saucepan; cook over medium heat until heated through, stirring occasionally.

5. Place tortillas in single layer on grid. Grill, uncovered, 1 to 2 minutes per side or until golden brown. (Pierce any tortillas which puff up with tip of knife or flatten by pressing with spatula.)

6. Transfer chicken and onions to cutting board. Slice chicken crosswise into ½-inch strips. Cut onions crosswise into 1-inch-long pieces. Spread tortillas with bean mixture; top with lettuce, chicken, onions, cheese, avocado and tomato. Sprinkle with cilantro and serve with sour cream, if desired. *Makes 4 servings*

Grilled Chicken Tostadas

Grilled Marinated Chicken

8 chicken leg quarters (about 3½ pounds)
6 ounces frozen lemonade concentrate, thawed
2 tablespoons white wine vinegar
1 tablespoon grated lemon peel
2 cloves garlic, minced

1. Remove skin and all visible fat from chicken. Place chicken in 13×9-inch glass baking dish. Combine lemonade concentrate, vinegar, lemon peel and garlic in small bowl; blend well. Pour over chicken; turn to coat. Cover; refrigerate 3 hours or overnight, turning occasionally.

2. Spray grid with nonstick cooking spray. Prepare grill for direct cooking.

3. Place chicken on grid over medium-high heat. Grill 20 to 30 minutes or until chicken is no longer pink near bone, turning occasionally. Garnish as desired.

Makes 8 servings

Mixed Grill

2 fennel bulbs, sliced lengthwise
1 large red bell pepper, cored, seeded and cut into large chunks
3 baby Japanese white eggplants *or* 2 small purple eggplants, cut into thick slices
3 plum tomatoes, cut into thick slices
3 large portobello mushrooms, wiped clean, stems removed and cut into thick slices
¼ cup light vinaigrette salad dressing
1 package (4 links) precooked chicken apple sausages
10 ounces boneless skinless chicken tenders
Lemon pepper
Black pepper
1 tablespoon fresh minced parsley

1. Spray grid with nonstick cooking spray. Prepare grill for direct cooking. Soak 8 wooden skewers in water 30 minutes.

2. Thread vegetables on bamboo skewers; sprinkle with salad dressing.

3. Slice sausages lengthwise; set aside. Season chicken with lemon pepper and black pepper; set aside.

4. Place vegetable skewers, chicken sausages and chicken tenders on hot grid. Cook 5 to 10 minutes, or until chicken reaches an internal temperature of 170°F. Sprinkle with parsley and serve.

Makes 8 servings

Grilled Marinated Chicken

Asian Chicken Kabobs

1 pound boneless skinless chicken breasts
2 small zucchini or yellow squash, cut into 1-inch slices
8 large fresh mushrooms
1 cup red, yellow or green bell pepper pieces
2 tablespoons reduced-sodium soy sauce
2 tablespoons dry sherry
1 teaspoon dark sesame oil
2 cloves garlic, minced
2 large green onions, cut into 1-inch pieces

1. Cut chicken into 1½-inch pieces; place in large resealable food storage bag. Add zucchini, mushrooms and bell pepper to bag. Combine soy sauce, sherry, oil and garlic in small bowl; pour over chicken and vegetables. Seal bag securely; turn to coat. Marinate in refrigerator at least 30 minutes or up to 4 hours.

2. Spray grid with nonstick cooking spray. Prepare grill for direct cooking. Soak 4 (12-inch) wooden skewers in water to cover 20 minutes.

3. Drain chicken and vegetables; reserve marinade. Alternately thread chicken and vegetables with onions onto skewers.

4. Place kabobs on grid. Brush with half of reserved marinade. Grill over medium heat 5 minutes. Turn kabobs over; brush with remaining marinade. Grill 5 minutes or until chicken is no longer pink. Garnish with green onion brushes, if desired.

Makes 4 serving

Asian Chicken Kabobs

Spiced Turkey with Fruit Salsa

6 ounces turkey breast tenderloin
2 teaspoons lime juice
1 teaspoon mesquite seasoning blend or ground cumin
½ cup frozen pitted sweet cherries, thawed and cut into halves*
¼ cup chunky salsa

*Drained canned sweet cherries can be substituted for frozen cherries.

1. Spray grid with nonstick cooking spray. Prepare grill for direct cooking. Brush both sides of turkey with lime juice. Sprinkle with mesquite seasoning.

2. Grill turkey over medium coals 15 to 20 minutes or until turkey is no longer pink in center, turning once.

3. Meanwhile, stir together cherries and salsa.

4. Thinly slice turkey. Spoon salsa mixture over turkey. *Makes 2 serving*

Cumin BBQ Chicken

1 cup barbecue sauce
½ cup orange juice
3 tablespoons vegetable oil
2 tablespoons minced garlic
2 teaspoons ground coriander
2 teaspoons ground cumin
1 teaspoon black pepper
½ teaspoon salt
2 whole chickens (about 3½ pounds each), cut up

1. Prepare grill for direct cooking.

2. Combine barbecue sauce, orange juice, oil, garlic, coriander, cumin, pepper and salt in medium bowl; mix well. Reserve ¾ cup sauce.

3. Place chicken on grid over medium heat. Grill, covered, 20 minutes, turning once. Brush lightly with remaining sauce. Grill about 20 minutes more or until chicken is cooked through (165°F). Serve with reserved sauce. *Makes 8 servings*

Spiced Turkey with Fruit Salsa

Grilled Chicken with Southern Barbecue Sauce

1 tablespoon vegetable or canola oil
½ cup chopped onion (about 1 small)
4 cloves garlic, minced
1 can (16 ounces) tomato sauce
¾ cup water
3 tablespoons packed light brown sugar
3 tablespoons chili sauce
2 teaspoons chili powder
2 teaspoons dried thyme
2 teaspoons Worcestershire sauce
¾ teaspoon ground red pepper
½ teaspoon cinnamon
½ teaspoon black pepper
6 skinless bone-in chicken breasts (2¼ pounds)

1. Heat oil in medium skillet over medium heat. Add onion and garlic; cook and stir about 5 minutes or until tender.

2. Stir in tomato sauce, water, brown sugar, chili sauce, chili powder, thyme, Worcestershire sauce, red pepper, cinnamon and black pepper; bring to a boil. Reduce heat to low and simmer, uncovered, 30 minutes or until mixture is reduced to about 1½ cups. Reserve ¾ cup sauce for basting. Meanwhile, prepare grill for indirect cooking.

3. Grill chicken, covered, over medium heat 40 to 45 minutes or until cooked through (165°F), turning chicken several times and basting occasionally with reserved sauce.

4. Heat remaining sauce in same skillet over medium heat; spoon over chicken.

Makes 4 servings

Hot Tip

The best way to determine doneness for grilled meats and poultry is to check the internal temperature with an instant-read thermometer. For chicken, insert the thermometer in the thickest part of the thigh, not touching the bone. The temperature should read 180°F. Another method to test doneness of chicken is to insert a fork into the thickest part of the piece. If the fork goes in easily, the juices are clear and the chicken is tender throughout, then it is fully cooked.

Grilled Chicken with Southern Barbecue Sauce

Thai Grilled Chicken

4 boneless chicken breasts (about 1¼ pounds), skinned if desired
¼ cup soy sauce
2 teaspoons minced garlic
½ teaspoon red pepper flakes
2 tablespoons honey
1 tablespoon fresh lime juice

1. Spray grid with nonstick cooking spray. Prepare grill for direct cooking. Place chicken in shallow baking dish. Combine soy sauce, garlic and pepper flakes in measuring cup. Pour over chicken, turning to coat. Let stand 10 minutes. Reserve marinade.

2. Meanwhile, combine honey and lime juice in small bowl until blended; set aside.

3. Place chicken on grid over medium coals; brush with reserved marinade. Discard remaining marinade. Grill, covered, 5 minutes. Brush both sides of chicken with honey mixture. Grill 5 minutes more or until chicken is no longer pink in center.

Makes 4 servings

Serving Suggestion: Serve with Oriental vegetables and fresh fruit salad.

Prep and Cook Time: 25 minutes

Hot Tip

Keep tongs or a spatula close by to turn meat and poultry on the grill. Stabbing the meat with a fork will drain the flavor-rich juices away.

Thai Grilled Chicken

Honey and Mustard Glazed Chicken

1 whole chicken (4 to 5 pounds)
1 tablespoon vegetable oil
¼ cup honey
2 tablespoons Dijon mustard
1 tablespoon reduced-sodium soy sauce
½ teaspoon ground ginger
⅛ teaspoon black pepper
   Dash salt

1. Prepare grill for indirect cooking.

2. Remove giblets from chicken cavity; reserve for another use or discard. Pull chicken skin over neck; secure with metal skewer. Tuck wings under back; tie legs together with kitchen string. Lightly brush chicken with oil.

3. Combine honey, mustard, soy sauce, ginger, pepper and salt in small bowl; set aside.

4. Place chicken, breast side up, on grid directly over drip pan. Grill, covered, over medium-high heat 1 hour 30 minutes or until cooked through (165°F) for both light and dark meat. Brush with honey mixture every 10 minutes during last 30 minutes of cooking time.*

5. Transfer chicken to cutting board; tent with foil. Let stand 15 minutes before carving. Internal temperature will continue to rise 5°F to 10°F during stand time.

Makes 4 to 6 servings

*If using grill with heat on one side (rather than around drip pan), rotate chicken 180 degrees after 45 minutes of cooking time.

Hot Tip

If the coals are too hot, raise the grill rack, spread the coals apart, close the air vents halfway or remove some briquets. For a gas or electric grill, adjust the burner to a lower setting.

Honey and Mustard Glazed Chicken

Spicy Island Chicken

1 cup finely chopped white onion
⅓ cup white wine vinegar
6 green onions, finely chopped
6 cloves garlic, minced
1 habañero or serrano pepper,* finely chopped
4½ teaspoons olive oil
4½ teaspoons fresh thyme *or* 2 teaspoons dried thyme
1 tablespoon ground allspice
2 teaspoons sugar
1 teaspoon salt
1 teaspoon ground cinnamon
1 teaspoon ground nutmeg
1 teaspoon black pepper
½ teaspoon ground red pepper
6 boneless skinless chicken breasts

*Chile peppers can sting and irritate the skin; wear rubber gloves when handling peppers and do not touch eyes. Wash hands after handling.

1. Combine all ingredients except chicken in medium bowl; mix well. Place chicken in large resealable food storage bag and add seasoning mixture. Seal bag; turn to coat chicken. Marinate in refrigerator 4 hours or overnight.

2. Spray cold grid with nonstick cooking spray. Adjust grid to 4 to 6 inches above heat. Prepare grill for direct cooking.

3. Remove chicken from marinade. Grill 5 to 7 minutes per side or until chicken is no longer pink in center, brushing occasionally with marinade. *Do not brush with marinade during last 5 minutes of grilling.* Discard remaining marinade.

Makes 6 servings

Spicy Island Chicken

Pesto-Stuffed Grilled Chicken

 2 cloves garlic, peeled
 ½ cup packed fresh basil
 2 tablespoons pine nuts or walnuts, toasted
 ¼ teaspoon black pepper
 5 tablespoons extra virgin olive oil, divided
 ¼ cup grated Parmesan cheese
 1 whole roasting chicken or capon (6 to 7 pounds)
 2 tablespoons fresh lemon juice

*To toast pine nuts, spread in single layer on baking sheet. Bake in preheated 350°F oven 8 to 10 minutes or until golden brown, stirring frequently.

1. Prepare grill with rectangular metal or foil drip pan. Bank briquets on either side of drip pan for indirect cooking.

2. Drop garlic through feed tube of food processor with motor running. Add basil, pine nuts and pepper; process until basil is minced. With processor running, add 3 tablespoons oil in slow, steady stream until smooth paste forms, scraping down side of bowl. Add cheese; process until well blended.

3. Remove giblets from chicken cavity; reserve for another use or discard. Loosen skin over breast of chicken by pushing fingers between skin and meat, taking care not to tear skin. Do not loosen skin over wings and drumsticks. Tuck wings under back; tie legs together with wet kitchen string. Using rubber spatula or small spoon, spread pesto under breast skin; massage skin to evenly spread pesto. Combine remaining 2 tablespoons oil and lemon juice in small bowl; brush over chicken skin.

4. Place chicken, breast side up, on grid directly over drip pan. Grill, covered, over medium-low heat 1 hour 10 minutes to 1 hour 30 minutes or until thermometer registers 165°F. Transfer chicken to cutting board; tent with foil. Let stand 15 minutes before carving. *Makes 6 servings*

Hot Tip

When cooking larger cuts of meat and poultry, such as a whole or quartered chicken, use the indirect method of grilling. Keep the grill tightly covered and resist the temptation to peek. Every time you lift the lid, you add 5 to 10 minutes to the cooking time.

Pesto-Stuffed Grilled Chicken

Smoked Turkey Breast with Chipotle Rub

Mesquite or hickory wood chips
2 tablespoons packed dark brown sugar
2 tablespoons ground cumin
1 tablespoon salt
1 tablespoon garlic powder
1 tablespoon smoked paprika
2 teaspoons ground chipotle pepper
1 teaspoon chili powder
4 tablespoons unsalted butter, softened
1 (5½- to 6-pound) bone-in skin-on turkey breast

1. Prepare grill for indirect cooking over medium-high heat. Soak wood chips in water at least 30 minutes.

2. Combine brown sugar, cumin, salt, garlic powder, paprika, chipotle and chili powder in small bowl; mix well. Place 2 tablespoons spice mixture in separate small bowl; mix with butter until well blended.

3. Gently loosen skin over turkey breast. Spread butter mixture under skin directly onto breast meat. Rub skin and cavity of turkey with remaining spice mixture.

4. Remove some wood chips from water; place in small aluminum tray. Place tray under grill rack directly on heat source and allow wood to begin to smolder, about 10 minutes.

5. Grill turkey, covered, 1 hour. Replenish wood chips after 1 hour. Grill until thermometer inserted into thickest portion registers 165°F. Transfer to cutting board; let stand 10 minutes before slicing.   *Makes 8 to 10 servings*

Smoked Turkey Breast with Chipotle Rub

Lemon Pepper Chicken

⅓ **cup lemon juice**
¼ **cup finely chopped onion**
¼ **cup olive oil**
1 **tablespoon brown sugar**
1 **tablespoon cracked black pepper**
3 **cloves garlic, minced**
2 **teaspoons grated lemon peel**
¾ **teaspoon salt**
4 **chicken quarters (about 2½ pounds)**

1. Combine lemon juice, onion, oil, sugar, pepper, garlic, lemon peel and salt in small bowl; reserve 2 tablespoons marinade. Combine remaining marinade and chicken in large resealable food storage bag. Seal bag; knead to coat. Refrigerate at least 4 hours or overnight.

2. Spray grid with nonstick cooking spray. Prepare grill for direct cooking.

3. Remove chicken from marinade; discard marinade. Transfer chicken to grill. Grill, covered, over medium-hot coals 15 to 20 minutes or until center is no longer pink, turning several times and basting often with reserved marinade.

Makes 4 servings

Hot Tip

A marinade is a seasoned liquid mixture that adds flavor and in some cases tenderizes. Always marinate in the refrigerator, never at room temperature. Never save and reuse a marinade.

Lemon Pepper Chicken

SIZZLING SEAFOOD

Grilled Salmon Fillets, Asparagus and Onions

 $^1/_2$ teaspoon paprika
 6 salmon fillets (6 to 8 ounces each)
 $^1/_3$ cup bottled honey-Dijon marinade or barbecue sauce
 1 bunch (about 1 pound) fresh asparagus spears, ends trimmed
 1 large red or sweet onion, cut into $^1/_4$-inch slices
 1 tablespoon olive oil
   Salt and black pepper

1. Spray grid with nonstick cooking spray. Prepare grill for direct cooking. Sprinkle paprika over salmon fillets. Brush mustard over salmon; let stand at room temperature 15 minutes.

2. Brush asparagus and onion slices with olive oil; season to taste with salt and pepper.

3. Place salmon, skin side down, in center of grid over medium coals. Arrange asparagus spears and onion slices around salmon. Grill salmon and vegetables on covered grill 5 minutes. Turn salmon, asparagus and onion slices. Grill 5 to 6 minutes more or until salmon flakes easily when tested with a fork and vegetables are crisp-tender. Separate onion slices into rings; arrange over asparagus.

Makes 6 serving.

Prep and Cook Time: 26 minutes

Grilled Salmon Fillet, Asparagus and Onions

Szechuan Tuna Steaks

4 tuna steaks (6 ounces each), cut 1 inch thick
¼ cup dry sherry or sake
¼ cup soy sauce
1 tablespoon dark sesame oil
1 teaspoon hot chili oil *or* ¼ teaspoon red pepper flakes
1 clove garlic, minced
3 tablespoons chopped fresh cilantro

1. Place tuna in single layer in large shallow baking dish. Combine sherry, soy sauce, sesame oil, hot chili oil and garlic in small bowl. Reserve ¼ cup marinade. Pour remaining marinade over tuna. Cover; marinate in refrigerator 40 minutes, turning once.

2. Spray grid with nonstick cooking spray. Prepare grill for direct cooking.

3. Drain tuna, discarding marinade. Place tuna on grid. Grill, uncovered, over medium-hot coals 6 minutes or until tuna is opaque, but still feels somewhat soft in center,* turning halfway through grilling time. Transfer tuna to carving board. Cut each tuna steak into thin slices; fan out slices onto serving plates. Drizzle tuna slices with reserved soy sauce mixture; sprinkle with cilantro. *Makes 4 servings*

*Tuna becomes dry and tough if overcooked. Cook it as if it were beef.

Hot Tip

Asian dark sesame oil is an amber-colored oil pressed from toasted sesame seeds. It has a strong, nutty flavor that when used sparingly adds a unique flavor to foods, such as stir-fries, Asian noodles and fish dishes.

Szechuan Tuna Steak

Mustard-Grilled Red Snapper

¹/₂ **cup Dijon mustard**
1 tablespoon red wine vinegar
1 teaspoon ground red pepper
4 red snapper fillets (about 6 ounces each)
    Fresh parsley sprigs and red peppercorns (optional)

1. Spray grid with nonstick cooking spray. Prepare grill for direct cooking.

2. Combine mustard, vinegar and pepper in small bowl; mix well. Coat fish thoroughly with mustard mixture.

3. Place fish on grid. Grill, covered, over medium-high heat 8 minutes or until fish flakes easily when tested with fork, turning halfway through grilling time. Garnish with parsley sprigs and red peppercorns.   *Makes 4 servings*

Hot Tip

Red snapper is a mild-flavored, low-fat fish. Try jazzing up red snapper with a tangy mustard coating before grilling it.

Mustard-Grilled Red Snapper

Lobster Tail with Tasty Butters

Hot & Spicy Butter, Scallion Butter or Chili-Mustard Butter (recipes follow)
4 fresh or thawed frozen lobster tails (about 5 ounces each)

1. Prepare grill for direct cooking. Prepare 1 butter mixture.

2. Rinse lobster tails in cold water. Butterfly tails by cutting lengthwise through centers of hard top shells and meat. Cut to, but not through, bottoms of shells. Press shell halves of tails apart with fingers. Brush lobster meat with butter mixture.

3. Place tails on grid, meat side down. Grill, uncovered, over medium-high heat 4 minutes. Turn tails meat side up. Brush with butter mixture and grill 4 to 5 minutes or until lobster meat turns opaque.

4. Heat remaining butter mixture, stirring occasionally. Serve butter sauce for dipping. *Makes 4 servings*

Tasty Butters

HOT & SPICY BUTTER
$1/3$ **cup butter or margarine, melted**
1 tablespoon chopped onion
2 to 3 teaspoons hot pepper sauce
1 teaspoon dried thyme leaves
$1/4$ **teaspoon ground allspice**

SCALLION BUTTER
$1/3$ **cup butter or margarine, melted**
1 tablespoon finely chopped green onion tops
1 teaspoon grated lemon peel
1 tablespoon lemon juice
$1/4$ **teaspoon black pepper**

CHILI-MUSTARD BUTTER
$1/3$ **cup butter or margarine, melted**
1 tablespoon chopped onion
1 tablespoon Dijon mustard
1 teaspoon chili powder

For each butter sauce, combine ingredients in small bowl.

Lobster Tail with Hot & Spicy Butter

Marinated Salmon with Lemon Tarragon Sauce

¼ cup lemon juice
¼ cup olive oil
2 cloves garlic, crushed
¾ teaspoon salt, divided
¼ teaspoon black pepper
1 pound fresh salmon fillet, 1-inch thick
⅔ cup sour cream
¼ cup minced green onions
¼ cup milk
1 teaspoon dried tarragon leaves *or* 1 tablespoon fresh tarragon leaves

1. Combine lemon juice, oil, garlic, ½ teaspoon salt and pepper in shallow, nonreactive 11×7-inch baking dish. Mix well. Add salmon; turn twice to coat. With salmon skin-side up in baking dish, cover tightly and refrigerate 2 hours.

2. Combine sour cream, green onions, milk, tarragon and remaining ¼ teaspoon salt in small bowl; mix well. Cover; refrigerate until ready to serve.

3. Spray grid with nonstick cooking spray. Prepare grill for direct cooking.

4. Cut salmon into 4 pieces. Grill over medium-high heat 5 minutes per side or until fish begins to flake when tested with fork. Serve with chilled sauce.

Makes 4 servings

Hot Tip

Oiling the fish's skin keeps it from sticking to the grill. If the fish fillet is thin, do not turn over. Cook skin side down until fish flakes easily with a fork and flesh is opaque.

Marinated Salmon with Lemon Tarragon Sauce

Grilled Halibut with Cherry Tomato Relish

2 cloves garlic, minced
3 tablespoons lemon juice, divided
2 teaspoons grated lemon peel, divided
2 teaspoons olive oil, divided
¼ teaspoon salt divided
¼ teaspoon black pepper, divided
4 halibut fillets (about 6 ounces each)
2 cups cherry tomatoes, quartered
2 tablespoons chopped fresh parsley

1. Combine garlic, 2 tablespoons lemon juice, 1 teaspoon lemon peel, 1 teaspoon oil, ⅛ teaspoon salt and ⅛ teaspoon pepper in large resealable food storage bag. Add halibut; seal bag and refrigerate 1 hour.

2. Combine tomatoes, parsley, remaining 1 tablespoon lemon juice, 1 teaspoon lemon peel, 1 teaspoon oil, ⅛ teaspoon salt and ⅛ teaspoon pepper in medium bowl; set aside.

3. Spray grid with nonstick cooking spray. Prepare grill for direct cooking.

4. Remove halibut from bag; discard marinade. Place halibut on grid; grill 3 to 5 minutes on each side or until fish begins to flake when tested with fork. Serve with relish.

Makes 4 servings

Prep Time: 15 minutes
Marinate Time: 1 hour
Grill Time: 6 to 10 minutes

Grilled Fish with Buttery Lemon Parsley

Nonstick cooking spray
6 tablespoons margarine
3 tablespoons finely chopped parsley
1 teaspoon grated lemon peel
½ teaspoon salt
½ teaspoon dried rosemary leaves
6 fish fillets, (6 ounces each) such as grouper, snapper or any lean white fish
3 medium lemons, halved

1. Spray cold grill rack with nonstick cooking spray. Prepare grill for direct cooking.

2. Combine margarine, parsley, lemon peel, salt and rosemary in small bowl; set aside.

3. Coat fish with cooking spray. Cook, uncovered, 3 minutes. Turn; grill 2 to 3 minutes longer or until opaque in center.

4. To serve, squeeze juice from 1 lemon half evenly over each fillet. Top with equal amounts of parsley mixture.   *Makes 6 servings*

Honey-Dijon Grilled Shrimp

¼ cup honey
¼ cup lemon juice
¼ cup orange juice
2 tablespoons Dijon-style mustard
½ teaspoon salt
¼ teaspoon white pepper
1 pound raw large shrimp, peeled and deveined
1 onion, cut into wedges
8 cherry tomatoes
2 limes, cut into wedges

1. Prepare grill for direct cooking. Combine honey, lemon juice, orange juice, mustard, salt and pepper in medium bowl; mix well.

2. Arrange shrimp, onion, tomatoes and limes in well-oiled wire grill basket; brush with marinade mixture.

3. Grill 4 to 6 minutes or until shrimp are pink and opaque, turning once and basting often with marinade mixture.   *Makes 4 servings*

Provençal Grilled Tuna Salad

4 (5- to 6-ounces each) tuna steaks, ¾ to 1 inch thick
3 tablespoons white wine or fish broth
3 tablespoons olive oil
2 tablespoons red wine vinegar
½ teaspoon chopped fresh rosemary *or* ¼ teaspoon dried rosemary leaves
½ teaspoon black pepper
⅛ teaspoon salt
1 clove garlic, minced
  Vegetable cooking spray
6 cups packed, torn salad greens
1 cup halved cherry tomatoes

Place fish in glass dish. To make vinaigrette, combine wine, oil, vinegar, rosemary, pepper and salt in jar with tight-fitting lid. Shake well. Pour 2 tablespoons vinaigrette over fish; add garlic and turn to coat. Marinate 15 to 30 minutes, turning once. Reserve remaining vinaigrette for salad dressing.

Coat grill rack with cooking spray and place on grill to heat 1 minute. Place tuna on grill 4 to 6 inches over hot coals. Cover with lid or tent with foil. Cook, turning once, just until tuna begins to flake easily when tested with fork, about 7 minutes. Discard marinade.

Meanwhile, arrange salad greens on 4 plates. Place hot tuna on greens and add cherry tomatoes. Shake remaining vinaigrette and drizzle over salads.

Makes 4 servings

Note: Halibut, swordfish or shark can be substituted for tuna.

Favorite recipe from **National Fisheries Institute**

Provençal Grilled Tuna Salad

Grilled Swordfish with Mango Salsa

1½ cups pineapple juice, divided
1 teaspoon minced fresh ginger, divided
2 pounds swordfish steaks, cut 1 inch thick
2 medium mangoes, peeled and coarsely chopped
4 kiwi, peeled and chopped
1 cup pineapple chunks
1 tablespoon brown sugar
1 tablespoon grated orange peel

1. Combine ¾ cup pineapple juice and ½ teaspoon ginger in small bowl; mix well.

2. Place fish in large resealable food storage bag. Pour pineapple juice mixture over fish; seal bag and turn to coat. Marinate in refrigerator about 2 hours, turning several times.

3. For salsa, combine remaining ¾ cup pineapple juice, ½ teaspoon ginger, mangoes, kiwi, pineapple chunks, brown sugar and orange peel in medium bowl. Cover and refrigerate until ready to serve.

4. Prepare grill for direct cooking. Remove fish from marinade; discard marinade. Grill fish, covered, over medium-high heat 5 minutes per side or until fish begins to flake when tested with fork. Serve with salsa. *Makes 6 servings*

Hot Tip

Allow about 10 minutes grilling time per inch thickness of fish fillets.

Grilled Swordfish with Mango Salsa

Garlic Skewered Shrimp

1 pound raw large shrimp, peeled and deveined
2 tablespoons reduced-sodium soy sauce
1 tablespoon vegetable oil
3 cloves garlic, minced
¼ teaspoon red pepper flakes (optional)
3 green onions, cut into 1-inch pieces

1. Prepare grill for direct cooking over medium heat. Soak 4 (12-inch) wooden skewers in hot water 30 minutes.

2. Meanwhile, place shrimp in large resealable food storage bag. Combine soy sauce, oil, garlic and red pepper flakes, if desired, in small bowl; mix well. Pour over shrimp. Seal bag; turn to coat. Marinate at room temperature 15 minutes.

3. Drain shrimp; reserve marinade. Alternately thread shrimp and green onions onto skewers. Brush with reserved marinade; discard any remaining marinade.

4. Grill skewers, covered, 5 minutes per side or until shrimp are pink and opaque.

Serving Suggestion: For a more attractive presentation, leave the tails on the shrimp.

Makes 4 serving

Hot Tip

When threading skewers, leave about a ¼-inch space between the pieces on the skewers to allow for even cooking.

Garlic Skewered Shrimp

Mesquite-Grilled Salmon Fillets

1 cup mesquite wood chips
2 tablespoons olive oil
1 clove garlic, minced
2 tablespoons lemon juice
1 teaspoon grated lemon peel
½ teaspoon dried dill weed
½ teaspoon dried thyme
¼ teaspoon salt
¼ teaspoon black pepper
4 salmon fillets, ¾ to 1 inch thick (about 5 ounces each)

1. Cover mesquite chips with cold water; soak 20 to 30 minutes. Spray grid with nonstick cooking spray. Prepare grill for direct cooking.

2. Combine oil and garlic in small microwavable bowl. Microwave at HIGH 1 minute or until garlic is tender. Add lemon juice, lemon peel, dill, thyme, salt and pepper; whisk until blended. Brush skinless sides of salmon with half of lemon mixture.

3. Drain mesquite chips; sprinkle chips over coals. Place salmon, skin side up, on grid. Grill, covered, over medium-high heat 4 to 5 minutes; turn and brush with remaining lemon mixture. Grill 4 to 5 minutes or until salmon flakes easily when tested with fork. *Makes 4 servings*

Hot Tip

For additional flavor, toss water-soaked wood chips, such as hickory or mesquite, onto ash-covered coals before adding food. Adding wood chips to the coals will create smoke which flavors the food. When cooking with wood chips, be sure the grill is in a well-ventilated area away from any open windows.

Mesquite-Grilled Salmon Fillet

Tuna Sicilian Style

¾ cup extra virgin olive oil
Juice of 2 lemons
4 cloves garlic, minced
1 tablespoon chopped fresh rosemary *or* 1½ teaspoons dried rosemary
1 tablespoon chopped fresh parsley
¾ teaspoon salt
½ teaspoon black pepper
4 fresh tuna steaks (½ inch thick)
Lemon slices (optional)
Arugula or spinach

1. Prepare grill for direct cooking.*

2. Combine oil, lemon juice, garlic, rosemary, parsley, salt and pepper in small bowl. Set aside half of basting sauce until ready to serve. Brush both sides of tuna with some of remaining sauce.

3. Place tuna on grid over medium-high heat. Grill 4 minutes, basting generously with sauce. Turn and grill 4 to 6 minutes or until desired degree of doneness, brushing frequently with sauce. Add lemon slices to grill for last few minutes, if desired.

4. Transfer tuna to serving dish lined with arugula; keep warm. Heat reserved sauce in small saucepan over low heat. Drizzle sauce over fish and greens just before serving. Garnish with lemon slices. *Makes 4 servings*

*Tuna may also be prepared on stovetop grill pan.

Tuna Sicilian Style

Mediterranean Red Snapper

4 sheets (18×12 inches) heavy-duty foil
1 to 1½ pounds red snapper fillets (4 to 5 ounces each)
8 sun-dried tomatoes, packed in oil, drained and chopped
⅓ cup sliced ripe olives
1½ teaspoons minced garlic
½ teaspoon dried oregano
½ teaspoon dried marjoram
¼ teaspoon black pepper
⅛ teaspoon salt

1. Prepare grill for direct cooking. Spray foil with nonstick cooking spray.

2. Place one fish fillet in center of each sheet of foil.

3. Combine tomatoes, olives, garlic, oregano, marjoram, pepper and salt in small bowl; mix well. Spoon evenly over fish.

4. Double-fold sides and ends of foil to seal packets, leaving head space for heat circulation. Place packets on baking sheet.

5. Slide packets off baking sheet onto grid. Grill, covered, over medium-high heat 9 to 11 minutes or until fish begins to flake when tested with fork. Carefully open one end of each packet to allow steam to escape. Open packets completely and transfer fish to serving plates. *Makes 4 servings*

WINGS
& MORE

Table of
CONTENTS

Modern
CLASSICS

Appetizer Chicken Wings

2½ to 3 pounds (12 to 14) chicken wings
1 cup (8 ounces) fat-free French dressing
½ cup KARO® Light or Dark Corn Syrup
1 package (1.4 ounces) French onion soup, dip and recipe mix
1 tablespoon Worcestershire sauce

Cut tips from wings and discard. Cut wings apart at joints and arrange in 13×9×2-inch baking pan lined with foil.

In medium bowl, mix dressing, corn syrup, recipe mix and Worcestershire sauce; pour over wings.

Bake in 350°F oven 1 hour, stirring once, or until wings are tender.

Makes 24 servings

Prep Time: 15 minutes
Cook Time: 1 hour

Angel Wings

   1 can (10¾ ounces) condensed tomato soup, undiluted
   ¾ cup water
   ¼ cup packed brown sugar
2½ tablespoons balsamic vinegar
   2 tablespoons chopped shallots
   2 pounds chicken wings

SLOW COOKER DIRECTIONS

1. Combine soup, water, brown sugar, vinegar and shallots in slow cooker; mix well.

2. Add chicken; stir to coat with sauce. Cover; cook on LOW 5 to 6 hours.

Makes 4 to 6 servings

Roasted Rosemary Chicken

   ¼ cup finely chopped onion
   2 tablespoons or butter, melted
   1 tablespoon chopped fresh rosemary leaves *or* 1 teaspoon
      dried rosemary
   2 cloves garlic, minced
   ½ teaspoon salt
   ¼ teaspoon black pepper
   4 chicken leg quarters
   ¼ cup white wine or chicken broth

1. Preheat oven to 375°F.

2. Combine onion, butter, rosemary, garlic, salt and pepper in small bowl. Run finger under chicken skin to loosen. Rub onion mixture under and over skin. Place chicken, skin side up, in small shallow roasting pan. Pour wine over chicken.

3. Roast chicken 50 to 60 minutes or until browned and cooked through (165°F), basting occasionally with pan juices. *Makes 4 servings*

Game-Winning Drumsticks

15 chicken drumsticks (about 4 pounds)
1¾ cups SWANSON® Chicken Stock
½ cup Dijon-style mustard
⅓ cup Italian-seasoned dry bread crumbs

1. Put the chicken in a single layer in a 15×10-inch disposable foil pan.

2. Stir the stock and mustard in a small bowl. Pour the stock mixture over the chicken and turn to coat. Sprinkle the bread crumbs over the chicken. Cover the pan and refrigerate for 4 hours.

3. Bake at 375°F. for 1 hour or until the chicken is cooked through. Serve hot or at room temperature.   *Makes 6 servings*

Prep Time: 10 minutes
Marinate Time: 4 hours
Bake Time: 1 hour

Keep disposable foil pans on hand to conveniently tote food to friends' parties or covered dish suppers. As a safety reminder, be sure to support the bottom of the filled pan when placing them in and out of the oven.

Garlicky Gilroy Chicken Wings

1 cup olive oil, plus additional to grease baking pan
2 pounds chicken wings
2 heads garlic, separated into cloves and peeled*
1 teaspoon hot pepper sauce, or to taste
1 cup grated Parmesan cheese
1 cup Italian-seasoned dry bread crumbs
1 teaspoon black pepper
Ranch dip and celery sticks (optional)

*To peel whole heads of garlic, drop into boiling water for 5 to 10 seconds. Immediately remove garlic with slotted spoon. Plunge garlic into cold water; drain. Peel away skins.

1. Preheat oven to 375°F. Grease 13×9-inch nonstick baking pan with oil.

2. Rinse chicken under cold water; pat dry with paper towels. Remove and discard wing tips. Cut each wing in half at joint.

3. Place 1 cup oil, garlic and hot pepper sauce in food processor; process until smooth. Pour garlic mixture into small bowl. Combine Parmesan cheese, bread crumbs and black pepper in shallow dish. Dip chicken into garlic mixture, then roll in crumb mixture, coating evenly and shaking off excess.

4. Arrange chicken in single layer in prepared pan. Drizzle remaining garlic mixture over chicken; sprinkle with remaining crumb mixture. Bake 45 to 60 minutes or until chicken is browned and cooked through. Serve with ranch dip and celery sticks, if desired. *Makes 4 to 6 servings*

Cranberry-Barbecue Chicken Wings

3 pounds chicken wings
   Salt and black pepper
1 jar (12 ounces) cranberry-orange relish
½ cup barbecue sauce
2 tablespoons quick-cooking tapioca
1 tablespoon prepared mustard

SLOW COOKER DIRECTIONS

1. Preheat broiler. Rinse chicken wings under cold water; pat dry with paper towels. Remove and discard wing tips. Cut each wing in half at joint. Place chicken on rack of broiler pan; season with salt and pepper.

2. Broil 4 to 5 inches from heat 10 to 12 minutes or until browned, turning once. Transfer chicken to slow cooker.

3. Stir relish, barbecue sauce, tapioca and mustard in small bowl. Pour over chicken. Cover; cook on LOW 4 to 5 hours.   *Makes 6 to 8 servings*

Prep Time: 20 minutes
Cook Time: 4 to 5 hours

Hot 'n' Honeyed Chicken Wings

1 cup PACE® Picante Sauce
¼ cup honey
½ teaspoon ground ginger
12 chicken wings or chicken drummettes

1. Stir the picante sauce, honey and ginger in a small bowl.

2. Cut the chicken wings at the joints into 24 pieces. Discard the tips or save them for another use. Put the wings in a small bowl. Add the picante sauce mixture and toss to coat. Put the wings on a foil-lined shallow baking pan.

3. Bake at 400°F. for 55 minutes or until the wings are glazed and cooked through,* turning and brushing often with sauce during the last 30 minutes of cooking.   *Makes 24 appetizers*

The internal temperature of the chicken should reach 170°F.

Prep Time: 10 minutes
Bake Time: 55 minutes

Jerk Wings with Ranch Dipping Sauce

½ **cup mayonnaise**
½ **cup plain yogurt or sour cream**
1½ **teaspoons salt, divided**
1¼ **teaspoons garlic powder, divided**
½ **teaspoon black pepper, divided**
¼ **teaspoon onion powder**
2 **tablespoons orange juice**
1 **teaspoon sugar**
1 **teaspoon dried thyme**
1 **teaspoon paprika**
¼ **teaspoon ground nutmeg**
¼ **teaspoon ground red pepper**
2½ **pounds chicken wings**

1. Preheat oven to 450°F. Spray baking sheet with nonstick cooking spray.

2. Combine mayonnaise, yogurt, ½ teaspoon salt, ¼ teaspoon garlic powder, ¼ teaspoon black pepper and onion powder in small bowl. Cover; refrigerate until ready to serve.

3. Combine orange juice, sugar, thyme, paprika, nutmeg, red pepper, remaining 1 teaspoon salt, 1 teaspoon garlic powder and ¼ teaspoon black pepper in medium bowl.

4. Rinse chicken wings under cold water; pat dry with paper towels. Remove and discard wing tips. Cut each wing in half at joint. Add chicken to orange juice mixture; toss to coat.

5. Transfer chicken to prepared baking sheet. Bake 25 to 30 minutes or until skin is crisp and chicken is cooked through. Serve with dipping sauce.

Makes 4 to 6 servings

Salsa-Style Wings

1½ pounds chicken wings
2 cups prepared salsa
¼ cup brown sugar

1. Preheat oven to 350°F. Line 13×9-inch baking pan with foil. Rinse chicken wings under cold water; pat dry with paper towels. Remove and discard wing tips. Cut each wing in half at joint. Place chicken in even layer in prepared pan.

2. Stir salsa and brown sugar in medium bowl; pour over chicken.

3. Bake 1 hour or until chicken is cooked through, basting every 10 minutes with salsa mixture.

4. Serve with remaining salsa mixture from pan.   *Makes 4 servings*

Grilled Chicken Thighs

8 boneless, skinless chicken thighs
3 tablespoons MRS. DASH® Chicken Grilling Blends™
4 tablespoons red wine vinegar
2 tablespoons tomato paste
2 tablespoons honey
1 to 2 tablespoons water

Lay chicken thighs side by side in large glass casserole. Score each thigh 2 to 3 times using sharp knife.

Combine Mrs. Dash® Chicken Grilling Blends™, vinegar, tomato paste, honey and water. Set aside ¼ cup. Pour remaining marinade over chicken; marinate in refrigerator at least 1 hour.

Preheat grill to medium heat.

Brush thighs with reserved marinade and grill 10 minutes on each side.

Makes 4 servings

Prep Time: 5 minutes
Cook Time: 20 minutes

Hot Wings with Creamy Cool Dipping Sauce

Creamy Cool Dipping Sauce (page 275)
¼ cup chopped onion
2 tablespoons olive oil
2 cloves garlic, minced
1½ cups barbecue sauce
2 to 3 teaspoons hot pepper sauce
4 pounds chicken wings

1. Prepare grill for direct cooking.

2. Prepare Creamy Cool Dipping Sauce.

3. Place onion, oil and garlic in medium microwavable bowl. Microwave on HIGH 1½ to 2 minutes or until onion is tender. Add barbecue sauce and hot pepper sauce; stir until blended.

4. Rinse chicken wings under cold water; pat dry with paper towels. Remove and discard wing tips. Cut each wing in half at joint.

5. Grill chicken, covered, over medium-high heat 25 minutes or until cooked through, turning after 15 minutes. Turn and brush with barbecue sauce mixture during last 5 minutes of cooking. Serve with Creamy Cool Dipping Sauce.

Makes 8 to 10 servings

As soon as you get home with your groceries, immediately store the chicken in the coldest part of the refrigerator (40°F or below). Raw poultry can be refrigerated for up to two days. If the chicken you purchase will not be cooked within two days, it should be frozen.

Buffalo Chicken Drumsticks

3 tablespoons hot pepper sauce
1 tablespoon vegetable oil
1 clove garlic, minced
8 chicken drumsticks
¼ cup mayonnaise
3 tablespoons sour cream
1 tablespoon white wine vinegar
¼ teaspoon sugar
⅓ cup (about 1½ ounces) crumbled blue cheese
2 cups hickory chips
   Celery sticks

1. Combine hot pepper sauce, oil and garlic in large resealable food storage bag; add chicken. Seal bag; turn to coat. Marinate in refrigerator at least 1 hour, turning occasionally.

2. For blue cheese dressing, combine mayonnaise, sour cream, vinegar and sugar in medium bowl. Stir in cheese; cover and refrigerate until ready to serve.

3. Prepare grill for direct cooking. Meanwhile, cover hickory chips with cold water; soak 20 minutes. Drain chicken, discarding marinade. Drain hickory chips; sprinkle over coals.

4. Grill chicken, covered, over medium-high heat 25 to 30 minutes or until cooked through (165°F), turning occasionally. Serve with blue cheese dressing and celery sticks. *Makes 4 servings*

Tangy Baked Wings

1 envelope (about 1 ounce) dry onion soup and recipe mix
⅓ cup honey
2 tablespoons spicy brown mustard
18 chicken wings (about 3 pounds)

1. Stir the soup mix, honey and mustard in a large bowl.

2. Cut off the chicken wing ends and discard. Cut the chicken wings in half at the joint. Add the chicken to the soup mixture and toss to coat. Place the chicken into a large shallow-sided baking pan.

3. Bake at 400°F. for 45 minutes or until the chicken is cooked through, turning over once halfway through cooking time.   *Makes 36 appetizers*

Prep Time: 15 minutes
Bake Time: 45 minutes

The best way to defrost uncooked frozen chicken is to thaw it in its wrapping in the refrigerator. Allow enough time for it to thaw completely, about three to four hours per pound. Never defrost chicken on the countertop at room temperature. The outside of the chicken will thaw before the inside, increasing the possibility of harmful bacterial growth on the thawed portions.

Nutty Oven-Fried Chicken Drumsticks

- **1 cup cornflake crumbs**
- **⅓ cup finely chopped pecans**
- **1 tablespoon sugar**
- **1½ teaspoons salt**
- **½ teaspoon onion powder**
- **½ teaspoon black pepper**
- **12 chicken drumsticks**
- **1 egg**
- **¼ cup (½ stick) butter, melted**

1. Preheat oven to 400°F. Line baking sheet with foil.

2. Combine cornflake crumbs, pecans, sugar, salt, onion powder and pepper in large resealable food storage bag.

3. Beat egg in shallow bowl. Dip chicken in egg to coat.

4. Add chicken to crumb mixture, 2 pieces at a time; shake to coat.

5. Place chicken on prepared baking sheet; drizzle with butter. Bake 40 to 45 minutes or until cooked through (165°F). *Makes 4 servings*

It is much easier to chop nuts if they are warmed up a bit first. Heat them in the oven at 325°F for about 5 minutes or in the microwave on HIGH for 2 to 3 minutes.

Original Buffalo Chicken Wings

Zesty Blue Cheese Dip (page 276)
2½ pounds chicken wings, split and tips discarded
½ cup *Frank's® RedHot®* Original Cayenne Pepper Sauce (or to taste)
⅓ cup butter or margarine, melted
Celery sticks

1. Prepare Zesty Blue Cheese Dip.
2. Deep fry* wings at 400°F 12 minutes or until crisp and no longer pink; drain.
3. Combine *Frank's RedHot* Sauce and butter in large bowl. Add wings to sauce; toss well to coat evenly. Serve with Zesty Blue Cheese Dip and celery.

Makes 24 to 30 individual pieces

Or prepare wings using one of the cooking methods below. Add wings to sauce; toss well to coat evenly.

To Bake: Place wings in single layer on rack in foil-lined roasting pan. Bake at 425°F 1 hour or until crisp and no longer pink, turning once halfway through baking time.

To Broil: Place wings in single layer on rack in foil-lined roasting pan. Broil 6 inches from heat 15 to 20 minutes or until crisp and no longer pink, turning once halfway through cooking time.

To Grill: Place wings on oiled grid. Grill over medium heat 30 to 40 minutes or until crisp and no longer pink, turning often.

Shanghai Red Wings: Cook chicken wings as directed above. Combine ¼ cup soy sauce, 3 tablespoons honey, 3 tablespoons *Frank's RedHot* Sauce, 2 tablespoons peanut oil, 1 teaspoon grated peeled fresh ginger and 1 teaspoon minced garlic in small bowl. Mix well. Pour sauce over wings; toss well to coat evenly.

Santa Fe Wings: Cook chicken wings as directed above. Combine ¼ cup (½ stick) melted butter or margarine, ¼ cup *Frank's RedHot* Sauce, ¼ cup chili sauce and 1 teaspoon chili powder in small bowl. Mix well. Pour sauce over wings; toss well to coat evenly.

Sweet 'n' Spicy Wings: Cook chicken wings as directed above. Combine ⅓ cup *Frank's RedHot* Sauce, ¼ cup (½ stick) butter, 2 tablespoons each thawed frozen orange juice concentrate and honey, and ¼ teaspoon each ground cinnamon and ground allspice in small microwavable bowl. Microwave on HIGH 1 minute or until butter is melted. Stir until smooth. Pour sauce over wings; toss well to coat evenly.

Chicken Wings in Cerveza

1½ **pounds chicken wings or drumettes***
1 **teaspoon salt**
1 **teaspoon dried thyme**
⅛ **teaspoon black pepper**
1 **bottle (12 ounces) Mexican beer**

When using drumettes, simply place them in the marinade without cutting.

1. Rinse chicken wings under cold water; pat dry with paper towels. Remove and discard wing tips. Cut each wing in half at joint. Place chicken in shallow bowl; sprinkle with salt, thyme and pepper. Pour beer over chicken; toss to coat. Cover; marinate in refrigerator 2 hours or up to 6 hours.

2. Preheat oven to 375°F. Line shallow baking pan with foil; spray with nonstick cooking spray.

3. Drain chicken, reserving marinade. Arrange chicken in single layer on prepared pan. Bake 40 minutes or until chicken is browned and cooked through, turning and brushing with reserved marinade occasionally. *Do not brush with marinade during last 10 minutes of baking.* Discard remaining marinade.   *Makes 3 to 4 servings*

Wings are just the thing for a summer backyard bash or a casual game day get-together. Do a quick count of your guests and plan on having about 4 to 6 wings per person.

Honey-Mustard Chicken Wings

3 pounds chicken wings
1 teaspoon salt
1 teaspoon black pepper
½ cup honey
½ cup barbecue sauce
2 tablespoons spicy brown mustard
1 clove garlic, minced
3 to 4 thin lemon slices

SLOW COOKER DIRECTIONS

1. Preheat broiler. Rinse chicken wings under cold water; pat dry with paper towels. Remove and discard wing tips. Cut each wing in half at joint. Sprinkle with salt and pepper.

2. Place chicken on broiler rack; broil 4 to 5 inches from heat 10 minutes, turning halfway through cooking time. Place in slow cooker.

3. Combine honey, barbecue sauce, mustard and garlic in small bowl; mix well. Pour over chicken. Top with lemon slices. Cover; cook on LOW 4 to 5 hours.

4. Remove and discard lemon slices before serving.

Makes 6 to 8 servings

Prep Time: 20 minutes
Cook Time: 4 to 5 hours

Global FLAVORS

Moroccan-Spiced Chicken Wings

¼ cup orange juice
3 tablespoons tomato paste
2 teaspoons ground cumin
1 teaspoon salt
1 teaspoon curry powder
1 teaspoon ground turmeric
½ teaspoon ground cinnamon
½ teaspoon ground ginger
1 tablespoon olive oil
5 pounds chicken wings

SLOW COOKER DIRECTIONS

1. Combine orange juice, tomato paste, cumin, salt, curry powder, turmeric, cinnamon and ginger in large bowl; mix well.

2. Rinse chicken wings under cold water; pat dry with paper towels. Remove and discard wing tips. Cut each wing in half at joint.

3. Heat oil in large nonstick skillet over medium-high heat. Add chicken and brown in several batches, about 6 minutes per batch. Transfer chicken to bowl with sauce; toss to coat.

4. Transfer chicken to slow cooker. Cover; cook on LOW 6 to 7 hours or HIGH 3 to 3½ hours.   *Makes 10 to 12 servings*

Prep Time: 20 minutes
Cook Time: 6 to 7 hours (LOW) or 3 to 3½ hours (HIGH)

Mexican Drumsticks with Ranchero Dipping Sauce

12 chicken drumsticks (about 3 pounds)
1 packet (1.25 ounces) ORTEGA® Taco Seasoning Mix
1 bottle (8 ounces) ORTEGA® Taco Sauce
1 bottle (8 ounces) ranch dressing
1 cup ORTEGA® Original Salsa

PREHEAT oven to 350°F. Arrange drumsticks on baking pan. Sprinkle seasoning mix over drumsticks, turning to coat both sides.

BAKE 45 minutes; turn drumsticks over halfway through to bake evenly. Remove from oven.

PLACE taco sauce in large mixing bowl. Add drumsticks and toss to coat evenly. Replace on baking sheet; broil 4 minutes on each side or until crisp.

COMBINE ranch dressing and salsa to make dipping sauce. Serve with warm drumsticks. *Makes 12 appetizers*

Prep Time: 5 minutes
Start-to-Finish Time: 1 hour

Experiment with different flavors of ORTEGA® Taco Sauce for a spicier taste. Or try this recipe with chicken wings for a great alternative to traditional hot wings.

Soy-Braised Chicken Wings

2½ pounds chicken wings
¼ cup dry sherry
¼ cup soy sauce
3 tablespoons sugar
2 tablespoons cornstarch
2 tablespoons minced garlic, divided
2 teaspoons red pepper flakes
2 tablespoons vegetable oil
3 green onions, cut into 1-inch pieces
¼ cup chicken broth
1 teaspoon sesame oil
1 tablespoon sesame seeds, toasted*

*To toast sesame seeds, place in small skillet. Shake skillet over medium-low heat about 3 minutes or until seeds begin to pop and turn golden.

1. Rinse chicken wings under cold water; pat dry with paper towels. Remove and discard wing tips. Cut each wing in half at joint.

2. Combine sherry, soy sauce, sugar, cornstarch, 1 tablespoon garlic and red pepper flakes in large bowl; mix well. Reserve ¼ cup marinade. Add chicken to bowl. Cover; marinate in refrigerator overnight, turning once or twice.

3. Drain chicken; discard marinade. Heat wok or deep skillet over high heat 1 minute. Add 1 tablespoon vegetable oil; heat 30 seconds. Add half of chicken; cook 5 to 10 minutes or until browned, turning occasionally. Remove with slotted spoon to clean bowl. Repeat with remaining oil and chicken.

4. Add remaining 1 tablespoon garlic and green onions to wok; cook and stir 30 seconds. Add chicken and broth. Cover; cook 5 to 10 minutes or until chicken is cooked through, stirring occasionally.

5. Add sesame oil to reserved marinade; mix well. Pour over chicken in wok; cook and stir 2 minutes or until chicken is glazed with marinade. Transfer to serving platter; sprinkle with sesame seeds. *Makes 4 to 6 servings*

Ginger-Lime Chicken Thighs

⅓ **cup vegetable oil**
3 **tablespoons lime juice**
3 **tablespoons honey**
2 **teaspoons grated fresh ginger** *or* 1 **teaspoon ground ginger**
¼ **to** ½ **teaspoon red pepper flakes**
6 **boneless skinless chicken thighs**

1. Combine oil, lime juice, honey, ginger and red pepper flakes in small bowl. Pour ½ cup marinade into large resealable food storage bag. Add chicken. Seal bag; turn to coat. Marinate in refrigerator 30 to 60 minutes, turning occasionally.

2. Prepare grill for direct cooking.

3. Remove chicken from marinade; discard marinade. Grill chicken over medium-high heat 12 minutes or until cooked through, turning once. Brush with remaining marinade during last 5 minutes of cooking.

Makes 4 to 6 servings

West Indies Curried Drumsticks

12 **chicken drumsticks**
¾ **teaspoon salt, divided**
½ **teaspoon paprika**
1 **tablespoon cornstarch**
1 **tablespoon sugar**
1 **cup orange juice**
2 **cloves garlic, crushed**
1½ **teaspoons curry powder**
1 **teaspoon grated orange peel**
½ **teaspoon ground ginger**
½ **cup chopped cashews**

Place chicken in large baking dish; sprinkle with ½ teaspoon salt and paprika. Bake in 375°F oven 30 minutes. Mix cornstarch and sugar in small saucepan. Stir in orange juice, garlic, curry powder, orange peel, ginger and remaining ¼ teaspoon salt. Cook and stir over medium heat until mixture boils and thickens. Pour sauce over chicken; bake, basting once with pan juices, about 25 minutes more or until chicken is fork-tender. Sprinkle cashews over chicken.

Makes 6 servings

Favorite recipe from **Delmarva Poultry Industry, Inc.**

Thai Chicken Wings

5 pounds chicken wings
1 tablespoon peanut oil
½ cup coconut milk
1 tablespoon sugar
1 tablespoon Thai green curry paste
1 tablespoon fish sauce
¾ cup prepared spicy peanut sauce

SLOW COOKER DIRECTIONS

1. Rinse chicken wings under cold water; pat dry with paper towels. Remove and discard wing tips. Cut each wing in half at joint.

2. Heat oil in large nonstick skillet over medium-high heat. Add chicken and brown in several batches, about 6 minutes per batch. Transfer chicken to slow cooker.

3. Stir coconut milk, sugar, curry paste and fish sauce in small bowl until combined. Add to slow cooker. Cover; cook on LOW 6 to 7 hours or on HIGH 3 to 3½ hours. Drain cooking liquid. Stir in peanut sauce.

Makes 10 to 12 servings

Island Jerk Chicken Wings

1 cup Hawaiian barbecue sauce
1 can (6 ounces) crushed pineapple, drained
¼ cup packed brown sugar
2 tablespoons lime juice
1 clove garlic, chopped
½ teaspoon grated fresh ginger
     Hot pepper sauce (optional)
3 pounds chicken wings
2 tablespoons Caribbean jerk seasoning

1. Preheat oven to 350°F. Line baking sheet with foil. Combine barbecue sauce, pineapple, brown sugar, lime juice, garlic, ginger and hot pepper sauce, if desired, in food processor; process until well blended.

2. Rinse chicken wings under cold water; pat dry with paper towels. Remove and discard wing tips. Cut each wing in half at joint.

3. Place chicken on prepared baking sheet; rub with seasoning until well coated. Bake 20 minutes. Baste with sauce; bake 20 minutes or until cooked through.

Makes 6 to 8 servings

Coconut Chicken Tenders with Spicy Mango Salsa

- **1 firm ripe mango, peeled and chopped**
- **½ cup chopped red bell pepper**
- **3 tablespoons chopped green onions**
- **2 tablespoons chopped fresh cilantro**
- **Salt and ground red pepper**
- **1½ cups flaked coconut**
- **1 egg**
- **1 tablespoon vegetable oil**
- **¾ pound chicken tenders**

1. Combine mango, bell pepper, green onions and cilantro in small bowl. Season with salt and red pepper. Transfer half of salsa to food processor; process until almost smooth. Combine with remaining salsa.

2. Preheat oven to 400°F. Line baking sheet with foil. Spread coconut on prepared baking sheet; bake 5 minutes or until lightly browned, stirring every 2 minutes. Transfer coconut to food processor; process until finely chopped but not pasty.

3. Beat egg, oil and pinch of ground red pepper in small bowl. Add chicken; toss to coat. Roll chicken in coconut; place on same baking sheet. Bake 18 to 20 minutes or until chicken is cooked through. Serve with Spicy Mango Salsa.

Makes 2 to 3 servings

Chicken tenders or "supremes" are lean, tender strips found on the underside of the breast. They are skinless and boneless so they require little prep work and cook quickly.

Ginger Wings with Peach Dipping Sauce

Peach Dipping Sauce (page 277)
¼ cup soy sauce
2 cloves garlic, minced
1 teaspoon ground ginger
¼ teaspoon white pepper
2 pounds chicken wings

1. Preheat oven to 400°F. Line baking sheet with foil. Prepare Peach Dipping Sauce.

2. Combine soy sauce, garlic, ginger and pepper in large bowl. Rinse chicken wings under cold water; pat dry with paper towels. Remove and discard wing tips. Cut each wing in half at joint. Add chicken to soy sauce mixture; stir until well coated. Place chicken in single layer on prepared baking sheet.

3. Bake 40 minutes or until browned and cooked through, turning once. Serve with Peach Dipping Sauce. *Makes 4 to 6 servings*

Grilled Tandoori-Style Chicken Wings with Cucumber-Yogurt Sauce

3 pounds chicken wings
Cucumber-Yogurt Sauce (page 278)
Juice of 2 limes
2 tablespoons finely minced garlic
1 tablespoon finely minced fresh ginger
1 teaspoon *each* kosher salt, chili powder and garam masala

1. Rinse chicken wings under cold water; pat dry with paper towels. Remove and discard wing tips. Cut each wing in half at joint. Line baking sheet with foil. Prepare Cucumber-Yogurt Sauce.

2. Combine lime juice, garlic, ginger, salt, chili powder and garam masala in small bowl. Rub paste evenly over chicken. Cover; marinate in refrigerator 2 to 4 hours.

3. Preheat grill pan. Preheat oven to 350°F. Grill chicken until browned on all sides. Transfer chicken to prepared baking sheet.

4. Bake 35 to 40 minutes or until cooked through. Serve with Cucumber-Yogurt Sauce. *Makes 6 to 8 servings*

Chicken Bites with Orange-Walnut Sauce

½ cup orange marmalade
3 tablespoons orange juice
2 tablespoons chopped walnuts
2 pitted prunes, chopped
1 tablespoon raisins
¼ teaspoon black pepper, divided
2 boneless skinless chicken breasts, cut into 1-inch cubes
   Grated peel and juice of 1 orange
3 tablespoons olive oil, divided
2 tablespoons Spanish sherry
½ teaspoon salt

1. Combine marmalade, 3 tablespoons orange juice, walnuts, prunes, raisins and ⅛ teaspoon pepper in small microwavable bowl. Microwave on HIGH 1 minute; stir until blended.

2. Place chicken, orange peel, orange juice, 1 tablespoon oil, sherry, salt and remaining ⅛ teaspoon pepper in medium bowl; toss to coat.

3. Heat remaining 2 tablespoons oil in medium nonstick skillet over medium heat. Using slotted spoon, transfer chicken to skillet in 2 batches. Cook 5 minutes or until chicken is browned and cooked through. Add any remaining marinade. Bring to a boil; boil 1 minute. Transfer chicken to serving plate. Serve with Orange-Walnut Sauce. *Makes 4 to 6 servings*

Maple and Honey Wheat Beer Glazed Chicken Thighs

1 bottle (12 ounces) honey wheat beer, divided
⅔ cup orange juice, divided
¼ cup plus 2 tablespoons maple syrup, divided
2 tablespoons lemon juice
2 cloves garlic, minced
2 teaspoons grated fresh ginger, divided
6 chicken thighs
2 teaspoons cornstarch
2 teaspoons water
1¼ teaspoons salt
¼ teaspoon black pepper

1. Combine ¾ cup beer, ⅓ cup orange juice, 2 tablespoons maple syrup, lemon juice, garlic and 1 teaspoon ginger in large resealable food storage bag. Add chicken. Seal bag; turn to coat. Marinate in refrigerator 2 hours or overnight.

2. Combine remaining ¾ cup beer, ⅓ cup orange juice, ¼ cup maple syrup and 1 teaspoon ginger in small saucepan over medium-high heat; bring to a boil. Reduce heat to medium; simmer 4 minutes or until slightly thickened.

3. Whisk cornstarch and water in small bowl. Add cornstarch mixture, salt and pepper to saucepan; increase heat to high and boil 1 minute or until thickened. Remove from heat.

4. Prepare grill for indirect cooking. Remove chicken from marinade; discard marinade. Grill chicken, skin side down, 10 minutes. Turn and generously brush with glaze; grill 5 minutes. Repeat turning and brushing chicken 4 more times. Grill chicken 5 minutes after last application of glaze or until cooked through (165°F). *Makes 4 to 6 servings*

Ginger-Garlic Barbecued Turkey Wings

4 turkey wings

GINGER-GARLIC SAUCE
2 tablespoons light soy sauce
2 tablespoons dry sherry
1 tablespoon fresh gingerroot, finely chopped
1 teaspoon canola oil
1 teaspoon brown sugar
1 clove garlic, minced

1. Discard wing tips and divide wings into 2 pieces.

2. In large saucepan, cover turkey with water and bring to a boil. Simmer for 20 minutes.

3. Meanwhile, combine remaining ingredients to make Ginger-Garlic Sauce, stirring well to dissolve the sugar.

4. Remove turkey from water, and place in sauce to marinate in refrigerator for 2 to 12 hours.

5. Remove wings from sauce and grill over medium heat for 20 to 30 minutes, turning often. *Makes 4 servings*

Favorite recipe from **National Turkey Federation**

Chicken Drumettes with Chive-Caper Mayonnaise

⅓ **cup mayonnaise**
1 **tablespoon minced chives**
2 **teaspoons capers**
¼ **teaspoon black pepper, divided**
¼ **cup all-purpose flour**
½ **teaspoon paprika, divided**
¼ **teaspoon salt**
2 **eggs**
½ **cup plain dry bread crumbs**
1½ **pounds chicken drumettes**
2 **tablespoons butter**
2 **tablespoons vegetable oil**

1. Combine mayonnaise, chives, capers and ⅛ teaspoon pepper in small bowl. Cover; refrigerate until ready to serve.

2. Combine flour, ¼ teaspoon paprika, salt and remaining ⅛ teaspoon pepper in large resealable food storage bag. Beat eggs in large shallow bowl. Combine bread crumbs and remaining ¼ teaspoon paprika on large plate.

3. Rinse chicken drumettes under cold water; pat dry with paper towels. Add chicken to flour mixture; shake well to coat. Dip chicken in eggs, then roll in bread crumbs.

4. Heat butter and oil in large heavy skillet over medium-high heat until foam subsides. Cook chicken in batches 6 minutes or until browned, turning once. Reduce heat to low. Cook 5 minutes or until cooked through, turning once. Serve with Chive-Caper Mayonnaise.   *Makes 3 to 4 servings*

Gingered Chicken Thighs

1 tablespoon peanut or vegetable oil
½ teaspoon hot chili oil
8 chicken thighs
2 cloves garlic, minced
¼ cup sweet and sour sauce
1 tablespoon soy sauce
2 teaspoons minced fresh ginger
Cilantro (optional)
Orange peel (optional)

1. Heat peanut oil and chili oil in large nonstick skillet over medium-high heat. Cook chicken, skin side down, 4 minutes or until golden brown. Reduce heat to low; turn chicken. Cover; cook 15 to 18 minutes more or until cooked through (165°F). Drain fat.

2. Increase heat to medium. Add garlic; cook and stir 2 minutes. Combine sweet and sour sauce, soy sauce and ginger in small bowl. Brush half of mixture over chicken; turn and brush with remaining mixture. Cook 5 minutes or until sauce is thickened and chicken is cooked through, turning once.

3. Transfer chicken to serving platter; pour sauce over chicken. Garnish with cilantro and orange peel.   *Makes 4 to 6 servings*

Mahogany Wings

1 can (10½ ounces) CAMPBELL'S® Condensed Beef Broth
2 bunches green onions, chopped
1 cup soy sauce
1 cup plum sauce
6 cloves garlic, minced
½ cup light molasses or honey
¼ cup cider vinegar
6 pounds chicken wings
1 tablespoon cornstarch

SLOW COOKER DIRECTIONS

1. Stir the broth, onions, soy sauce, plum sauce, garlic, molasses and vinegar in a 6-quart slow cooker removable insert.*

2. Cut off the chicken wing tips and discard. Cut the chicken wings in half at the joint. Add the chicken to the cooker and stir to coat. Cover and refrigerate 6 hours or overnight.

3. Stir ½ **cup** of the marinade and cornstarch in a small bowl. Stir into the chicken mixture.

4. Cover and cook on HIGH for 4 to 5 hours** or until the chicken is cooked through.   *Makes 18 servings*

*If your slow cooker doesn't have a removable insert, you can stir the marinade ingredients into a large bowl instead. Add the chicken and stir to coat. Cover and refrigerate as directed. Pour the chicken mixture into the cooker and proceed with steps 3 and 4 as directed.

**Or on LOW for 7 to 8 hours.

Prep Time: 30 minutes
Marinate Time: 6 hours
Cook Time: 4 to 5 hours

Spicy Almond Chicken Drumettes

3 tablespoons vegetable oil
2 tablespoons jerk seasoning
½ teaspoon salt
3 pounds chicken drumettes
1 cup slivered almonds, finely chopped

1. Combine oil, seasoning and salt in small bowl; stir until blended. Place chicken in large bowl. Pour seasoning mixture over chicken; toss to coat. Cover; marinate in refrigerator 20 to 30 minutes.

2. Preheat oven to 400°F. Line large baking sheet with foil; spray with nonstick cooking spray.

3. Place almonds in shallow bowl. Roll chicken in almonds until coated. Transfer chicken to prepared baking sheet. Bake 30 to 35 minutes or until chicken is cooked through. *Makes 6 to 8 servings*

Grilled Vietnamese-Style Chicken Wings

3 pounds chicken wings
⅓ cup honey
¼ to ⅓ cup sliced lemongrass
¼ cup fish sauce
2 tablespoons chopped garlic
2 tablespoons minced shallots
2 tablespoons chopped fresh ginger
2 tablespoons *each* lime juice and canola oil

1. Rinse chicken wings under cold water; pat dry with paper towels. Remove and discard wing tips. Cut each wing in half at joint.

2. Combine honey, lemongrass, fish sauce, garlic, shallots, ginger, lime juice and oil in food processor; process until smooth. Pour marinade into large resealable food storage bag. Add chicken. Seal bag; toss to coat. Marinate in refrigerator 4 hours or overnight.

3. Preheat grill pan. Preheat oven to 350°F. Line baking sheet with foil. Remove chicken from marinade; reserve marinade. Grill chicken 7 to 10 minutes or until browned, basting occasionally with marinade. Discard any remaining marinade.

4. Transfer chicken to prepared baking sheet; bake 20 to 30 minutes or until cooked through. *Makes 6 to 8 servings*

Asian Barbecue Skewers

2 pounds boneless skinless chicken thighs
½ cup soy sauce
⅓ cup packed brown sugar
2 tablespoons sesame oil
3 cloves garlic, minced
½ cup thinly sliced green onions (optional)
1 tablespoon toasted sesame seeds (optional)

SLOW COOKER DIRECTIONS

1. Cut each thigh into 4 pieces. Thread onto 7-inch wooden skewers, folding thinner pieces if necessary. Place skewers in slow cooker, layering as flat as possible.

2. Combine soy sauce, brown sugar, oil and garlic in small bowl. Reserve ⅓ cup sauce. Pour remaining sauce over skewers. Cover; cook on LOW 2 hours. Turn skewers; cook 1 hour.

3. Transfer skewers to serving platter. Discard cooking liquid. Pour reserved sauce over skewers; sprinkle with green onions and sesame seeds, if desired.

Makes 4 to 6 servings

Prep Time: 10 minutes
Cook Time: 3 hours

Toasted sesame seeds enhance the flavor of foods and add a little crunch. To toast, place 2 tablespoons sesame seeds and ½ teaspoon of oil in a microwavable dish. Heat on HIGH 1½ to 2½ minutes or just until very light brown, stirring seeds once or twice during cooking. Let stand 2 minutes. Repeat if necessary.

Oriental Chicken Wings

3 pounds chicken wings
1 cup chopped red onion
1 cup soy sauce
¾ cup packed light brown sugar
¼ cup dry sherry
2 tablespoons chopped fresh ginger
2 cloves garlic, minced
   Chopped fresh chives (optional)

SLOW COOKER DIRECTIONS

1. Rinse chicken wings under cold water; pat dry with paper towels. Remove and discard wing tips. Cut each wing in half at joint. Preheat broiler. Line baking sheet with foil; spray with nonstick cooking spray.

2. Transfer chicken to prepared baking sheet. Broil 5 minutes per side. Transfer to slow cooker.

3. Combine onion, soy sauce, brown sugar, sherry, ginger and garlic in medium bowl until well blended. Pour over chicken.

4. Cover; cook on LOW 5 to 6 hours or on HIGH 2 to 3 hours. Sprinkle with chives, if desired.

Makes 6 to 8 servings

Chipotle Orange BBQ Drumsticks

½ cup barbecue sauce, preferably mesquite or hickory smoked
1 to 2 tablespoons minced canned chipotle peppers in adobo sauce
1 teaspoon grated orange peel
8 chicken drumsticks
1 teaspoon ground cumin

1. Spray grid with nonstick cooking spray. Prepare grill for direct cooking.

2. Combine barbecue sauce, chipotle peppers and orange peel in small bowl.

3. Sprinkle chicken evenly with cumin.

4. Grill chicken, covered, over medium-high heat 30 to 35 minutes or until cooked through (165°F), turning frequently. Baste with sauce during last 5 minutes of cooking, turning and basting frequently until all of sauce is used.

Makes 4 to 6 servings

Marinated Thai Turkey Wings

4 turkey wings

THAI MARINADE
  ½ cup smooth peanut butter
  ½ cup water
  3 tablespoons light soy sauce
  3 tablespoons fresh lemon juice
  2 tablespoons brown sugar
  2 green onions, chopped
  3 drops hot pepper sauce

1. Discard wing tips and divide wings into 2 pieces.

2. In large saucepan, cover turkey with water and bring to a boil. Simmer for 20 minutes.

3. Meanwhile, combine remaining ingredients to make Thai Marinade, stirring well to dissolve sugar.

4. Remove turkey from water and place in marinade to marinate in refrigerator for 2 to 12 hours.

5. Remove wings from marinade and grill over medium heat for 20 to 30 minutes, turning often. *Makes 4 servings*

Favorite recipe from **National Turkey Federation**

Bombay Chicken Wings

2 (1¼-pound) packages chicken wing drummettes (24 pieces)
1 teaspoon curry powder
½ teaspoon ground turmeric
2 tablespoons soy sauce
2 tablespoons vegetable oil
2 tablespoons minced green onion
2 cloves garlic, minced
⅛ teaspoon black pepper
  Sprigs of cilantro for garnish
  Yogurt Chutney Dipping Sauce (page 274)

In large bowl, mix all ingredients except chicken wings and cilantro to make marinade. Add chicken wings, making sure all pieces are coated well with mixture; cover and refrigerate for at least 1 hour.

Prepare Yogurt Chutney Dipping Sauce. Preheat oven to 350°F. Drain chicken wings; place in single layer on jelly-roll pan. Bake 25 minutes until golden brown. Arrange on platter surrounding a bowl of Yogurt Chutney Dipping Sauce. Garnish with cilantro sprigs and serve. *Makes 24 appetizers*

Favorite recipe from **National Chicken Council**

Spicy Korean Chicken Wings

½ **cup reduced-sodium soy sauce**
¼ **cup cider vinegar**
¼ **cup honey**
¼ **cup chili garlic sauce**
2 **tablespoons orange juice**
1 **tablespoon sesame oil**
2 **tablespoons peanut oil, plus additional for frying**
2 **tablespoons grated fresh ginger**
3 **pounds chicken wings**
  Sesame seeds (optional)

1. Combine soy sauce, vinegar, honey, chili garlic sauce, orange juice and sesame oil in large bowl until blended. Heat 2 tablespoons peanut oil in large skillet over medium-high heat. Add ginger; cook and stir 2 minutes. Add soy sauce mixture; cook and stir 2 minutes. Remove from heat; set aside.

2. Rinse chicken wings under cold water; pat dry with paper towels. Remove and discard wing tips. Cut each wing in half at joint.

3. Heat 2 inches peanut oil in large heavy saucepan over medium-high heat until 350°F to 375°F, adjusting heat to maintain temperature.

4. Add chicken; cook 8 to 10 minutes or until browned and cooked through. Transfer to paper towels.

5. Add chicken to sauce; toss to coat. Sprinkle with sesame seeds, if desired.

Makes 6 to 8 servings

Bar Food
BITES

Ortega® Hot Poppers

1 can (3½ ounces) ORTEGA® Whole Jalapeños, drained
1 cup (4 ounces) shredded Cheddar cheese
1 package (3 ounces) cream cheese, softened
¼ cup chopped fresh cilantro
½ cup all-purpose flour
2 eggs, lightly beaten
2 cups cornflake cereal, crushed
  Vegetable oil
  ORTEGA® Salsa, any variety
  Sour cream

CUT jalapeños lengthwise into halves; remove seeds.

BLEND Cheddar cheese, cream cheese and cilantro in small bowl. Place 1 to 1½ teaspoons cheese mixture into each jalapeño half; chill for 15 minutes or until cheese is firm.

DIP each jalapeño half in flour; shake off excess. Dip in eggs; coat with cornflake crumbs.

ADD vegetable oil to 1-inch depth in medium skillet; heat over high heat for 1 minute. Fry jalapeños, turning frequently with tongs, until golden brown on all sides. Remove from skillet; drain on paper towels. Serve with salsa and sour cream.

Makes 8 servings

Oven-Fried Chicken Tenders

¾ cup vegetable oil
1 cup buttermilk
1 egg, beaten
1 cup all-purpose flour
2 to 3 teaspoons Cajun seasoning
¾ teaspoon paprika
½ teaspoon garlic powder
1½ pounds chicken tenders
    Salt and black pepper

1. Pour oil into large roasting pan; place pan in cold oven. Preheat oven to 425°F.

2. Whisk buttermilk and egg in medium bowl until well blended. Combine flour, Cajun seasoning, paprika and garlic powder in shallow baking dish or pie plate. Coat chicken with flour mixture. Dip into buttermilk mixture; coat again with flour mixture. Place on plate in single layer. (If chicken begins to absorb flour, coat with flour mixture again.)

3. Place coated chicken in heated oil in roasting pan in oven; bake 6 minutes. Turn; bake 6 minutes or until chicken is golden and cooked through. Place chicken on serving platter; season with salt and pepper.

Makes 6 to 8 servings

Buffalo-Style Chicken Nachos

2 cups diced cooked chicken
⅓ cup *Frank's® RedHot®* Original Cayenne Pepper Sauce
2 tablespoons melted butter
1 bag (10 ounces) tortilla chips
3 cups shredded Cheddar or Monterey Jack cheese

1. Preheat oven to 350°F. Combine chicken, **Frank's RedHot** Sauce and butter. Layer chips, chicken and cheese in ovenproof serving dish or baking dish.

2. Bake 5 minutes or just until cheese melts. Garnish as desired. Splash on more **Frank's RedHot** Sauce to taste.

Makes 4 servings

Spicy Grilled Quesadillas

8 flour tortillas (8 inch)
2 cups shredded Cheddar cheese (about 8 ounces)
1 jar (16 ounces) PACE® Chunky Salsa
1 cup diced cooked chicken
4 medium green onions, chopped (about ½ cup)
  Vegetable oil
1 container (8 ounces) sour cream

1. Top **each** of **4** tortillas with ½ **cup** cheese, ¼ **cup** salsa, ¼ **cup** chicken and **2 tablespoons** green onions. Brush the edges of the tortillas with water. Top with the remaining tortillas and press the edges to seal.

2. Lightly oil the grill rack and heat the grill to medium. Brush the tops of the quesadillas with oil. Place the quesadillas oil-side down on the grill rack. Brush the other side of the quesadillas with oil. Grill the quesadillas for 5 minutes or until the cheese is melted, turning the quesadillas over once during grilling. Remove the quesadillas from the grill and let stand 2 minutes.

3. Cut the quesadillas into wedges. Serve with the remaining salsa and sour cream.
Makes 4 servings

Prep Time: 10 minutes
Cook Time: 5 minutes
Stand Time: 2 minutes

Quesadillas are an easy way to turn leftover meat and shredded cheese into a whole new meal. You can even combine different varieties of shredded cheese to make the 2 cups needed in this recipe.

Barbecue Chicken Sliders

1 pound ground chicken
½ cup barbecue sauce, divided
Nonstick cooking spray
4 slices sharp Cheddar cheese, quartered (optional)
4 to 6 slices whole wheat sandwich bread
Lettuce leaves

1. Combine chicken and ¼ cup barbecue sauce in medium bowl. Shape mixture into 16 meatballs.

2. Spray large skillet or nonstick grill pan with cooking spray; heat over medium-high heat. Place meatballs in skillet; press with spatula to form patties. Cook patties 6 minutes per side or until cooked through (165°F). Top with cheese, if desired.

3. Meanwhile, toast bread and cut into circles or quarters.

4. Top bread with lettuce and patties; serve with remaining barbecue sauce.

Makes 16 servings

Raspberry-Balsamic Glazed Meatballs

1 bag (34 ounces) frozen fully cooked meatballs
1 cup raspberry preserves
3 tablespoons sugar
3 tablespoons balsamic vinegar
1½ tablespoons Worcestershire sauce
¼ teaspoon red pepper flakes
1 tablespoon grated fresh ginger (optional)

SLOW COOKER DIRECTIONS

1. Coat slow cooker with nonstick cooking spray. Add frozen meatballs.

2. Combine preserves, sugar, vinegar, Worcestershire sauce and red pepper flakes in small microwavable bowl. Microwave on HIGH 45 seconds. Stir; microwave 15 seconds or until melted (mixture will be chunky). Reserve ½ cup mixture. Pour remaining mixture over meatballs and toss to coat. Cover; cook on LOW 5 hours or on HIGH 2½ hours.

3. *Turn slow cooker to HIGH.* Stir in ginger, if desired, and reserved ½ cup preserves mixture. Cook, uncovered, 15 to 20 minutes or until thickened slightly, stirring occasionally.

Makes 4 servings

Chicken Satay Skewers

    6 garlic cloves, chopped
    4 teaspoons dried coriander
    4 teaspoons light brown sugar
    2 teaspoons salt
 1½ teaspoons HERSHEY₅S Cocoa
    1 teaspoon ground black pepper
    ½ cup soy sauce
    6 tablespoons vegetable oil
    2 tablespoons lime juice
    4 teaspoons fresh chopped ginger
 2½ pounds boneless, skinless chicken breasts
    Peanut Dipping Sauce (page 275)
    ¼ cup fresh cilantro, chopped (optional)

1. Combine garlic, coriander, brown sugar, salt, cocoa and pepper in large bowl. Stir in soy sauce, oil, lime juice and ginger.

2. Cut chicken into 1½- to 2-inch cubes. Add to soy sauce mixture, stirring to coat chicken pieces. Cover; marinate in refrigerator for at least 2 hours.

3. Meanwhile, prepare Peanut Dipping Sauce. Thread chicken pieces onto skewers. Grill or broil, basting with marinade. Discard leftover marinade. Garnish with chopped cilantro, if desired. Serve with Peanut Dipping Sauce. Refrigerate leftovers.   *Makes 15 to 20 appetizers or 4 to 6 entrée servings*

Baked Sweet Potato Fries with Spicy Apricot Dipping Sauce

    3 sweet potatoes (12 to 14 ounces each), peeled and cut into narrow
       wedges
    2 tablespoons vegetable oil
 1½ teaspoons kosher salt
    ¼ teaspoon black pepper
    Spicy Apricot Dipping Sauce (page 274)

1. Preheat oven to 450°F. Gently toss potatoes, oil, salt and pepper in large bowl until evenly coated. Divide potatoes between 2 large baking sheets. Bake 30 minutes or until lightly browned.

2. Prepare Spicy Apricot Dipping Sauce. Serve potatoes with sauce.

Makes 6 servings

Cheesy Chicken Nachos

2 tablespoons olive oil
1 onion, diced
1 teaspoon POLANER® Chopped Garlic
1 pound ground chicken
1 jar (16 ounces) ORTEGA® Salsa, any variety, divided
2 teaspoons dried parsley
1 teaspoon ORTEGA® Chili Seasoning Mix
1 teaspoon REGINA® Red Wine Vinegar
½ cup water
12 ORTEGA® Yellow Corn Taco Shells, broken
1 pound shredded taco cheese blend (4 cups)
1 can (15 ounces) JOAN OF ARC® Black Beans
1 jar (12 ounces) ORTEGA® Sliced Jalapeños

HEAT oil in skillet over medium-high heat until hot. Add onion and garlic. Cook and stir until onion is translucent, about 3 minutes. Stir in chicken, ¾ cup salsa, parsley, seasoning mix, vinegar and ½ cup water; cook until meat is cooked through and sauce begins to thicken, about 5 minutes.

PREHEAT broiler; place rack about 7 inches from top of oven.

ASSEMBLE nachos by arranging broken taco shells on baking sheet. Sprinkle on 2 cups cheese; top with chicken mixture, black beans and jalapeños. Add remaining salsa and cheese. (If desired, prepare individual portions by dividing recipe among 6 heat-resistant plates.)

PLACE under broiler 4 minutes or until cheese begins to melt.

Makes 6 servings

Prep Time: 10 minutes
Start-to-Finish Time: 20 minutes

Note: Be sure to have some of your favorite guacamole, sour cream and black olives on hand to place on top of the nachos.

Substitution: If you have ground beef on hand, you can still make these tasty nachos. Just brown the meat first and discard the excess fat before proceeding as directed. Or try this recipe with ground turkey.

Crispy Mozzarella Sticks

**1 package (17.3 ounces) PEPPERIDGE FARM® Frozen Puff
   Pastry Sheets (2 sheets)**
1 egg
1 tablespoon water
1 package (12 ounces) mozzarella cheese snack sticks (12 sticks)
¼ cup grated Parmesan cheese
1 cup PREGO® Marinara Italian Sauce

1. Thaw the pastry sheets at room temperature for 30 minutes or until they're easy to handle. Heat the oven to 400°F. Beat the egg and water in a cup with a fork.

2. Unfold **1** pastry sheet on a lightly floured surface. Cut the pastry into 6 (5×3-inch) rectangles. Repeat with the remaining pastry sheet.

3. Put a mozzarella stick on the long edge of each pastry rectangle and roll up in the pastry. Press the pastry gently along the long edge and pinch the ends to seal.

4. Brush the tops of pastry rolls with the egg mixture. Dip the tops in the Parmesan cheese and place the rolls cheese-side up on an ungreased baking sheet 1 inch apart. Prick the tops of the pastry rolls with a fork 6 times down the length of each roll.

5. Bake for 17 minutes or until golden. (Some cheese may ooze out.)

6. Heat the sauce in a 1½-quart saucepan over medium heat until warm, stirring occasionally. Serve the rolls with the sauce for dipping.

Makes 12 servings

Sloppy "Cup of Joe" Sliders

- **1 tablespoon vegetable oil**
- **1 onion, halved and sliced**
- **1 green bell pepper, halved and sliced**
- **1½ pounds ground beef**
- **1½ cups spicy barbecue sauce (not mesquite)**
- **½ cup ketchup**
- **1 teaspoon instant coffee granules**
- **1 package (16½ ounces) sweet Hawaiian dinner rolls**
- **½ cup shredded Monterey Jack cheese**

1. Heat oil in large skillet over medium heat. Add onion and pepper; cook and stir 10 minutes or until softened but not browned. Remove from skillet; set aside.

2. Brown beef in same skillet 6 to 8 minutes, stirring to break up meat. Drain fat. Return beef to skillet; stir in barbecue sauce, ketchup and coffee granules. Reduce heat to medium-low; simmer 10 minutes.

3. Slice dinner rolls in half. Place about ⅓ cup sloppy joe mixture on bottom halves of rolls. Top with 1 tablespoon cheese and ¼ cup onions and peppers. Top with top halves of rolls; microwave on HIGH 15 seconds or until cheese is melted. *Makes 10 sandwiches*

Spinach, Crab and Artichoke Dip

1 package (10 ounces) frozen chopped spinach, thawed and squeezed nearly dry
1 package (8 ounces) cream cheese
1 jar (6 to 7 ounces) marinated artichoke hearts, drained and finely chopped
1 can (6½ ounces) crabmeat, drained and shredded
¼ teaspoon hot pepper sauce
  Melba toast or whole grain crackers (optional)

SLOW COOKER DIRECTIONS
Combine spinach, cream cheese, artichoke hearts, crabmeat and hot pepper sauce in slow cooker. Cover; cook on HIGH 1½ to 2 hours or until heated through, stirring after 1 hour. (Dip will stay warm in slow cooker for 2 hours.) Serve with melba toast, if desired.   *Makes 10 servings*

Tex-Mex Potato Skins

3 hot baked potatoes, split lengthwise
¾ cup (3 ounces) shredded Cheddar or pepper Jack cheese
1⅓ cups *French's*® French Fried Onions, divided
¼ cup chopped green chiles
¼ cup crumbled cooked bacon
  Salsa and sour cream

1. Preheat oven to 350°F. Scoop out insides of potatoes, leaving ¼-inch shells. Reserve insides of potatoes for another use.

2. Arrange potato halves on baking sheet. Top with cheese, ⅔ *cup* French Fried Onions, chiles and bacon.

3. Bake 15 minutes or until heated through and cheese is melted. Cut each potato half crosswise into thirds. Serve topped with salsa, sour cream and remaining onions.   *Makes 18 appetizer servings*

Prep Time: 15 minutes
Cook Time: 15 minutes

Tip: To bake potatoes quickly, microwave at HIGH 10 to 12 minutes or until tender.

Pork Tenderloin Sliders

   2 teaspoons chili powder
   ¾ teaspoon ground cumin
   ½ teaspoon salt
   ½ teaspoon black pepper
   2 tablespoons olive oil, divided
   2 pork tenderloins (about 1 pound each)
   12 green onions
   ½ cup mayonnaise
   1 chipotle pepper in adobo sauce, minced
   2 teaspoons lime juice
   12 dinner rolls
   12 slices Monterey Jack cheese

1. Prepare grill for direct cooking.

2. Combine chili powder, cumin, salt and black pepper in small bowl. Rub 1 tablespoon oil evenly over tenderloins. Sprinkle seasoning mixture evenly over tenderloins, coating all sides. Place green onions and remaining 1 tablespoon oil in large resealable food storage bag; seal bag. Knead to coat onions with oil.

3. Combine mayonnaise, chipotle pepper and lime juice in small bowl until well blended. Cover; refrigerate until ready to serve.

4. Grill tenderloins, covered, 15 to 20 minutes or until cooked through (160°F), turning occasionally. Remove to cutting board. Tent with foil; let stand 10 minutes.

5. Meanwhile, grill green onions 3 minutes or until browned, turning occasionally. Cool slightly; coarsely chop.

6. Thinly slice tenderloins. Spread chipotle mayonnaise on cut sides of rolls. Serve pork on rolls with green onions and cheese.   *Makes 12 sandwiches*

Buffalo Chicken Tenders

    3 tablespoons Louisiana-style hot pepper sauce
    ½ teaspoon paprika
    ¼ teaspoon ground red pepper
    1 pound chicken tenders
    ½ cup blue cheese dressing
    ¼ cup sour cream
    2 tablespoons crumbled blue cheese
    1 green or red bell pepper, cut lengthwise into
        ½-inch slices

1. Preheat oven to 375°F. Spray 11×7-inch baking dish with nonstick cooking spray. Combine hot pepper sauce, paprika and red pepper in small bowl; brush over chicken. Place chicken in prepared baking dish. Cover; marinate in refrigerator 30 minutes.

2. Bake 15 minutes or until chicken is cooked through.

3. Combine blue cheese dressing, sour cream and blue cheese in small serving bowl. Serve chicken with dip and bell pepper slices.

Makes 4 to 6 servings

Pizza Fries

    1 bag (2 pounds) frozen French fries
    1 cup PREGO® Traditional Italian Sauce, any variety
  1½ cups shredded mozzarella cheese (about 6 ounces)
       Diced pepperoni (optional)

1. Prepare the fries according to the package directions. Remove from the oven. Pour the sauce over the fries.

2. Top with the cheese and pepperoni, if desired.

3. Bake for 5 minutes or until the cheese is melted.   *Makes 8 servings*

Prep Time: 20 minutes
Bake Time: 5 minutes

Three Pepper Quesadillas

1 cup *each* thin green, red and yellow bell pepper strips
½ cup thin onion slices
⅓ cup butter or margarine
½ teaspoon ground cumin
1 package (8 ounces) PHILADELPHIA® Cream Cheese, softened
1 package (8 ounces) KRAFT® Shredded Sharp Cheddar Cheese
10 TACO BELL® HOME ORIGINALS® Flour Tortillas
1 jar (16 ounces) TACO BELL® HOME ORIGINALS®* Thick 'N Chunky Salsa

PREHEAT oven to 425°F. Cook and stir peppers and onion in butter in large skillet on medium-high heat until crisp-tender. Stir in cumin. Drain, reserving liquid.

BEAT cream cheese and Cheddar cheese with electric mixer on medium speed until well blended. Spoon 2 tablespoons cheese mixture onto each tortilla; top each evenly with pepper mixture. Fold tortillas in half; place on ungreased baking sheet. Brush with reserved liquid.

BAKE 10 minutes or until heated through. Cut each tortilla into thirds. Serve warm with salsa. *Makes 30 servings*

Prep Time: 20 minutes
Bake Time: 10 minutes

Make Ahead: Prepare as directed except for baking; cover. Refrigerate. When ready to serve, bake, uncovered, at 425°F, 15 to 18 minutes or until heated through.

Chicken Fingers with Dijonaise Dipping Sauce

DIJONAISE DIPPING SAUCE
- 3 tablespoons mayonnaise
- 2 tablespoons honey Dijon mustard
- 1 tablespoon lemon juice

CHICKEN FINGERS
- ¾ cup **CREAM OF WHEAT**® Hot Cereal (Instant, 1-minute, 2½-minute or 10-minute cook time), uncooked
- ¾ cup grated Parmesan cheese
- ¾ teaspoon ground paprika
- ¼ cup milk
- 2 eggs
- 4 boneless skinless chicken breasts (1 pound)
- Nonstick cooking spray

1. Combine all sauce ingredients in small bowl; set aside until ready to use.

2. Preheat oven to 450°F. Coat baking sheet with nonstick cooking spray. Combine Cream of Wheat, cheese and paprika in shallow bowl; set aside. Combine milk and eggs in second shallow bowl; set aside.

3. Flatten chicken breasts slightly to uniform thickness. Cut into strips. Dip each strip into Cream of Wheat mixture, coating evenly. Dip into egg mixture, coating evenly. Dip into Cream of Wheat mixture again, coating evenly. Place strips on prepared baking sheet. Lightly coat strips with cooking spray. Bake 6 minutes; turn over strips and bake 6 minutes longer. Serve with Dijonaise Dipping Sauce or your favorite dipping sauce. *Makes 4 servings*

Prep Time: 10 minutes
Start-to-Finish Time: 25 minutes

Taco Chili Fries

1 bag (16 ounces) frozen French fries
2 pounds lean ground beef
1½ cups water
2 packets (1.25 ounces each) ORTEGA® Taco Seasoning Mix
1 cup ORTEGA® Salsa, any variety
1 can (15 ounces) JOAN OF ARC® black beans, drained
1 can (6 ounces) sliced black olives, drained
1 can (4 ounces) ORTEGA® Diced Green Chiles
2 cups (8 ounces) shredded Cheddar cheese
1 cup sour cream (optional)

FOLLOW package directions for baking fries. Set aside.

BROWN ground beef in medium skillet over medium-high heat. Stir in water and seasoning mix. Cook 5 minutes. Remove from heat.

SPOON salsa, beans, olives, chiles, cheese and sour cream, if desired, into separate bowls. Place fries in large bowl near meat mixture and toppings. Using heat-resistant ceramic plates, allow guests to create their own chili fries with meat and toppings. (Reserve sour cream until after mixture has been broiled.)

PLACE ceramic plate under broiler about 4 minutes or until fries reheat and cheese melts. Top with sour cream, if desired. Serve immediately.

Makes 6 servings

Prep Time: 15 minutes
Start-to-Finish Time: 45 minutes

Note: Try using a variety of cheeses, from a jalapeño-Cheddar or Monterey Jack to a stout blue cheese. Or offer a selection of diced fresh vegetables to top these chili fries.

One-Bite Burgers

1 package (11 ounces) refrigerated breadstick dough (12 breadsticks)
1 pound ground beef
2 teaspoons hamburger seasoning mix
9 slices Cheddar or American cheese, quartered (optional)
36 round dill pickle slices

1. Preheat oven to 375°F. Separate dough into 12 breadsticks; cut each breadstick into 3 equal pieces. Working with 1 piece at a time, tuck ends under to meet at center, pressing to seal and form very small bun about 1½ inches in diameter and ½ inch high.

2. Place buns seam side down on ungreased baking sheet. Bake 11 to 14 minutes or until golden brown. Remove to wire racks.

3. Meanwhile, combine beef and seasoning in large bowl. Shape into 36 patties, using about 2 teaspoons per patty.

4. Heat large skillet over medium heat. Cook patties 7 minutes or until cooked through, turning once. Top with cheese slice, if desired.

5. Split buns in half crosswise. Serve burgers on buns with pickle slices.

Makes 36 mini burgers

Buffalo-Style Wraps

⅔ cup *Frank's® RedHot®* Original Cayenne Pepper Sauce, divided
4 boneless skinless chicken breast halves
¼ cup blue cheese salad dressing
1 cup shredded lettuce
1 cup (4 ounces) shredded Monterey Jack cheese
4 (10-inch) flour tortillas, heated

1. Combine ⅓ *cup* **Frank's RedHot** Sauce and *1 tablespoon oil* in resealable plastic food storage bag. Add chicken. Seal bag; toss to coat evenly. Marinate in refrigerator 30 minutes or overnight.

2. Broil or grill chicken 10 to 15 minutes or until no longer pink in center. Slice chicken into long thin strips. In bowl, toss chicken with remaining ⅓ *cup* **Frank's RedHot** Sauce and dressing.

3. Arrange chicken, lettuce and cheese down center of tortillas, dividing evenly. Fold bottom third of each tortilla over filling; fold sides towards center. Tightly roll up to secure filling. Cut in half to serve.   *Makes 4 servings*

Prep Time: 10 minutes
Cook Time: 10 minutes

Dips, Spreads
& SAUCES

Velveeta® Spicy Buffalo Dip

**1 pound (16 ounces) VELVEETA® Pasteurized Prepared Cheese
    Product, cut into ½-inch cubes**
1 cup BREAKSTONE'S® or KNUDSEN® Sour Cream
¼ cup cayenne pepper sauce for Buffalo wings
¼ cup KRAFT® Natural Blue Cheese Crumbles
2 green onions, sliced

COMBINE VELVEETA®, sour cream and pepper sauce in large microwaveable bowl. Microwave on high 5 minutes or until VELVEETA® is completely melted, stirring after 3 minutes.

STIR in remaining ingredients.

SERVE hot with celery and carrot sticks.   *Makes 2¾ cups dip*

Prep Time: 5 minutes
Total Time: 10 minutes

Variation: Prepare as directed, using VELVEETA® Made With 2% Milk Reduced Fat Pasteurized Prepared Cheese Product and BREAKSTONE'S® Reduced Fat or KNUDSEN® Light Sour Cream.

Serve It Cold: This dip is also great served cold. Prepare as directed; cool. Cover and refrigerate several hours or until chilled. Serve as directed.

Keeping It Safe: Hot dips should be discarded after sitting at room temperature for 2 hours or longer.

Yogurt Chutney Dipping Sauce

½ cup plain yogurt
3 tablespoons mango, finely chopped
1 tablespoon cilantro, minced
1 tablespoon green onion, minced
¼ teaspoon hot pepper sauce
⅛ teaspoon salt

In medium bowl, combine all ingredients; cover and refrigerate until needed.

Makes ¾ cup sauce

Favorite recipe from **National Chicken Council**

Asian Honey Mustard Dressing

¾ cup mayonnaise
2 tablespoons rice wine vinegar
2 tablespoons honey
2 tablespoons prepared mustard
1 teaspoon soy sauce
1 teaspoon dark sesame oil

Combine mayonnaise, vinegar, honey, mustard, soy sauce and sesame oil in medium bowl; mix well.

Makes 1 cup dressing

Spicy Apricot Dipping Sauce

1 cup apricot jam
¼ cup orange juice
1 tablespoon prepared mustard
¼ teaspoon ground red pepper

Melt jam in small saucepan over medium-high heat. Whisk in orange juice, mustard and red pepper. Process in food processor or with immersible blender until smooth.

Makes about 1¼ cups sauce

Peanut Dipping Sauce

½ cup peanut oil
1 cup REESE'S® Creamy Peanut Butter
¼ cup lime juice
¼ cup soy sauce
3 tablespoons honey
2 garlic cloves, minced
1 teaspoon cayenne pepper
½ teaspoon hot pepper sauce

Gradually whisk peanut oil into peanut butter in medium bowl. Blend in lime juice, soy sauce, honey, garlic, cayenne pepper and hot pepper sauce. Adjust flavors to taste for a sweet/hot flavor.   *Makes 2¼ cups sauce*

Creamy Cool Dipping Sauce

⅔ cup mayonnaise
¼ cup ranch dressing
3 ounces crumbled feta cheese
2 teaspoons finely chopped green onion

Combine mayonnaise and salad dressing in small bowl. Stir in cheese and green onion. Cover and refrigerate until ready to serve.

Makes 1¼ cups sauce

Zesty Blue Cheese Dip

½ cup blue cheese salad dressing
¼ cup sour cream
2 teaspoons *Frank's*® *RedHot*® Original Cayenne Pepper Sauce

Combine all ingredients in medium serving bowl; mix well. Garnish with crumbled blue cheese, if desired. *Makes ¾ cup dip*

Prep Time: 5 minutes

Barbecue Bacon Party Spread

2 packages (8 ounces each) PHILADELPHIA® Cream Cheese, softened
¼ cup KRAFT® THICK 'N SPICY® Original Barbecue Sauce
1 package (2.8 ounces) OSCAR MAYER® Real Bacon Recipe Pieces
1 small tomato, chopped
½ cup chopped green bell pepper
⅓ cup sliced green onions
1½ cups KRAFT® Shredded Cheddar Cheese
TRISCUIT® Thin Crisps sliced green onions

SPREAD cream cheese on large platter; drizzle with barbecue sauce. Top with all remaining ingredients except the Thin Crisps. Serve with the Thin Crisps. *Makes 35 servings*

Peach Dipping Sauce

½ **cup peach preserves**
2 **tablespoons light corn syrup**
1 **teaspoon white vinegar**
¼ **teaspoon ground ginger**
¾ **teaspoon soy sauce**

Combine preserves, corn syrup, vinegar and ginger in small saucepan. Cook and stir over medium-high heat until mixture simmers. Remove from heat; stir in soy sauce. Cool to room temperature.   *Makes ½ cup sauce*

Buttermilk Ranch Dressing

¾ **cup mayonnaise**
½ **cup buttermilk**
2 **tablespoons chopped fresh chives**
1 **tablespoon chopped fresh Italian parsley**
1 **clove garlic, minced**
1 **teaspoon salt**
½ **teaspoon black pepper**

Whisk mayonnaise, buttermilk, chives, parsley, garlic, salt and pepper in small bowl. Refrigerate 30 minutes before serving.   *Makes 1¼ cups dressing*

Cucumber-Yogurt Sauce

1 container (7 ounces) plain Greek-style yogurt
½ seedless cucumber, peeled and grated
1½ tablespoons chopped fresh mint
1 tablespoon lemon juice
1 clove garlic, minced
Salt and black pepper

Combine yogurt, cucumber, mint, lemon juice, garlic, salt and pepper in medium bowl until well blended. Cover; refrigerate until ready to serve.

Makes 1½ cups sauce

Barbecue Dipping Sauce

1 can (15 ounces) CONTADINA® Pizza Sauce
¼ cup firmly packed brown sugar
2 tablespoons vinegar
1 tablespoon prepared mustard
½ teaspoon liquid smoke

1. Combine pizza sauce, brown sugar, vinegar, mustard and liquid smoke in medium saucepan.
2. Bring to a boil. Reduce heat to low; simmer, uncovered, for 5 minutes, stirring occasionally. Serve with chicken nuggets, meatballs, shrimp or cocktail franks, if desired.

Makes about 2 cups sauce

Prep Time: 3 minutes
Cook Time: 5 minutes

The publisher would like to thank the companies and organizations listed below for the use of their recipes and photographs in this publication.

ACH Food Companies, Inc.

American Lamb Council

Australian Lamb

The Beef Checkoff

Campbell Soup Company

Cream of Wheat® Cereal

Del Monte Foods

Delmarva Poultry Industry, Inc.

The Hershey Company

Holland House®

Jennie-O Turkey Store, LLC

Kraft Foods Global, Inc.

McIlhenny Company (TABASCO® brand Pepper Sauce)

Mrs. Dash® SALT-FREE SEASONING BLENDS

National Chicken Council / US Poultry & Egg Association

National Fisheries Institute

National Honey Board

National Pork Board

National Turkey Federation

Newman's Own, Inc.®

North Dakota Beef Commission

Ortega®, A Division of B&G Foods, Inc.

Recipes courtesy of the Reynolds Kitchens

Reckitt Benckiser Inc.

Sargento® Foods Inc.

Unilever

Metric Conversion Chart

VOLUME MEASUREMENTS (dry)

⅛ teaspoon = 0.5 mL
¼ teaspoon = 1 mL
½ teaspoon = 2 mL
¾ teaspoon = 4 mL
1 teaspoon = 5 mL
1 tablespoon = 15 mL
2 tablespoons = 30 mL
¼ cup = 60 mL
⅓ cup = 75 mL
½ cup = 125 mL
⅔ cup = 150 mL
¾ cup = 175 mL
1 cup = 250 mL
2 cups = 1 pint = 500 mL
3 cups = 750 mL
4 cups = 1 quart = 1 L

VOLUME MEASUREMENTS (fluid)

1 fluid ounce (2 tablespoons) = 30 mL
4 fluid ounces (½ cup) = 125 mL
8 fluid ounces (1 cup) = 250 mL
12 fluid ounces (1½ cups) = 375 mL
16 fluid ounces (2 cups) = 500 mL

WEIGHTS (mass)

½ ounce = 15 g
1 ounce = 30 g
3 ounces = 90 g
4 ounces = 120 g
8 ounces = 225 g
10 ounces = 285 g
12 ounces = 360 g
16 ounces = 1 pound = 450 g

DIMENSIONS

1/16 inch = 2 mm
⅛ inch = 3 mm
¼ inch = 6 mm
½ inch = 1.5 cm
¾ inch = 2 cm
1 inch = 2.5 cm

OVEN TEMPERATURES

250°F = 120°C
275°F = 140°C
300°F = 150°C
325°F = 160°C
350°F = 180°C
375°F = 190°C
400°F = 200°C
425°F = 220°C
450°F = 230°C

BAKING PAN SIZES

Utensil	Size in Inches/Quarts	Metric Volume	Size in Centimeters
Baking or Cake Pan (square or rectangular)	8×8×2	2 L	20×20×5
	9×9×2	2.5 L	23×23×5
	12×8×2	3 L	30×20×5
	13×9×2	3.5 L	33×23×5
Loaf Pan	8×4×3	1.5 L	20×10×7
	9×5×3	2 L	23×13×7
Round Layer Cake Pan	8×1½	1.2 L	20×4
	9×1½	1.5 L	23×4
Pie Plate	8×1¼	750 mL	20×3
	9×1¼	1 L	23×3
Baking Dish or Casserole	1 quart	1 L	—
	1½ quart	1.5 L	—
	2 quart	2 L	—